A Paste

Harlequins Rugby

Paul Fletcher and Philip Gordos

London League Publications Ltd

A Pastel Revolution

Harlequins Rugby League – The Inside Story

Front cover photo: Solomon Haumono charging forward against Castleford Tigers (photo: David Williams – rlphotos.com)
Back: The players and the Harlequin Hearts after the last match of the season against Salford City Reds (photo: Peter Lush)

A CIP catalogue record for this book is available from the British Library.

First published in Great Britain in November 2006 by:
London League Publications Ltd, P.O. Box 10441, London E14 8WR

ISBN (10): 1-903659-29-9
ISBN: (13) 978-1903659-29-8
Cover design by: Stephen McCarthy Graphic Design
46, Clarence Road, London N15 5BB

Editorial & Layout: Peter Lush

Printed and bound by: Biddles Ltd
King's Lynn, Great Britain

London League Publications Ltd would like to thank Harlequins RL for their co-operation in the production of this book and for providing access to players and staff. However, the views expressed in the book are those of the individuals concerned, and are not necessarily those of Harlequins RL.

Foreword

I have got nothing but admiration for everyone connected with Harlequins Rugby League. They have fought long and hard to make the club a success, often overcoming extreme odds to prevail. But now it looks like their loyalty and dedication is paying off. The future is finally starting to look rosy and it's about time their story was told.

I'm delighted for David Hughes, who has dreamed of a successful and prosperous club in London. He dug deep into his pockets when it mattered most and fought tooth and nail to keep the club alive when others were trying to obliterate it. He deserves any success that comes his way.

Thanks and credit must also go to Nic Cartwright, Tony Rea, Chris Warren, the players and the fans. Without their efforts, the club would probably not have survived either. I take my hat off to their fighting spirit.

I applaud Ian Lenagan, too, for deciding to get involved with the club. As chairman and joint owner, he is absolutely the right man to take it forward. His business acumen and pure passion for the game make him a major asset. He has already made some smart moves that will benefit the club in the long run.

Everyone realises this is an exciting time for Harlequins Rugby League and nothing has pleased me more than seeing this club come to life. Its fans should feel proud of the club and what it has achieved. I wish it every success.

Mike Stephenson

A Great Britain international who played a starring role for Dewsbury and Australian side Penrith, Mike 'Stevo' Stephenson is now a leading commentator on rugby league, and is an expert summariser for Sky Sports.

Thank you

We would like to thank all the people at Harlequins Rugby League and everyone else who assisted and helped with the writing of this book, in particular Dom Fenton, Nic Cartwright and Chris Warren; Caroline Ellis and Kate Gordos for all their support and patience over the last 10 months; Robert Pendlebury, who provided a laptop for Paul when his broke down at a vital stage; Michael O'Hare for sub-editing, Steve McCarthy for designing the cover, David Williams for supplying photos, the staff of Biddles for printing the book and Peter Lush and Dave Farrar for their backing and hard work.

About the authors

Philip Gordos, 36, is a sports journalist for the BBC. He started his career as a part-time football reporter on the *Walsall Chronicle* before moving to the *Newport Advertiser* in Shropshire. He covered Telford United and Shrewsbury Town for the *Shropshire Star*, then West Bromwich Albion for the *Evening Mail* and *Sports Argus* in Birmingham. He joined the fledgling BBC Sport website in June 2000 and has covered a wide range of events, from the 2000 Rugby League World Cup to the 2004 Olympic Games in Athens. He lives with his wife, Kate, and three sons, Ben, Luke and Harry, in south-east London. Born and brought up in Wolverhampton, this is his second book. He co-wrote *Kevin Sinfield: Life with Leeds Rhinos, A 2003 Rugby League Diary*.

Paul Fletcher, 33, is a sports journalist for the BBC. He started his career at a press agency in Leeds, covering the fortunes of a number of football clubs in the north of England as well as reporting on the 2000 European Football Championships. He moved to London in 2001 and specialises in both football and rugby league for the BBC Sport website. He has covered numerous big events, notably the 2004 European Championships in Portugal and the 2006 World Cup in Germany. He also reported on the Ashes in 2003 as well as rugby league's Tri-Nations Series in 2004 and 2005. A columnist for the *Lancashire Evening Post* newspaper, Paul lives in west London with his girlfriend, Caroline, and is desperate to see Preston North End reach the Premiership.

Contents

"You can have anything you want, if you want it badly enough. You can be anything you want to be, do anything you set out to accomplish if you hold to that desire with singleness of purpose."

Abraham Lincoln
16th President of the United States of America

1. New beginnings

"It is a positive day for the club but a miserable day for the team."
Tony Rea, Harlequins RL coach

It was with a heavy heart that Harlequins RL coach Tony Rea faced the press after his team's 40-16 home loss to St Helens on the opening weekend of Super League XI. Dressed appropriately in black, the Australian spoke frankly of his disappointment to the handful of journalists who had gathered in the media room deep in the bowels of The Twickenham Stoop's Lexus Stand.

Rea's assessment of his team's display was brutal. He gave it a 0/10 rating. But he was also realistic. This was, after all, only the first game of the 2006 season and it was too early to start panicking. However, Rea knew a golden opportunity had been wasted. The club had attached great significance to the game against Saints. It was the first competitive fixture as Harlequins RL following the transformation from the London Broncos and represented the dawn of a bright, new era, one that many hoped would finally see the club blossom into a potent rugby league force.

Most Harlequins RL supporters realised it was asking a lot for the team to beat St Helens. Daniel Anderson's side were the pre-competition favourites, boasting such stellar players as Jamie Lyon, Sean Long, Paul Wellens and Jason Cayless. But a decent performance in defeat would have gone a long way to winning over those fans who regarded the move to the Stoop to co-habit with a rugby union club with a great deal of trepidation. Instead, the home side had looked nervous, tentative and anything but a cohesive outfit. They proved to be no match for a Saints side who showed remarkable ruthlessness so early in the season.

Recognising that the day had not panned out as he or the club had hoped, Rea made a heartfelt plea to the thousands of Harlequins RL fans who had trooped dejectedly from the ground in the wake of the seven-try reverse on Saturday 11 February. "I would like people to give us a second chance," he urged. "I'm disappointed and so are the team."

The build-up to the clash with St Helens had inevitably focused on the club's innovative tie-up with NEC Harlequins. The exciting cross-code partnership - cemented on 26 July 2005 - had divided opinion across the rugby league world and proved to be a hot topic among the rugby union fraternity too. There had been co-operation between the rival codes in the past - at Leeds, for example - but this development took it to a whole new level. For the extremists on either side, it was an alliance that bordered on the treacherous. But for those who felt the antagonism that existed between league and union should be confined to the history books, it was a breath of fresh air.

As one might expect, supporters of the London Broncos had had plenty to say about their shock and, some would say, controversial metamorphosis. Having started off life as Fulham 26 years earlier, the club's short history was already littered with more dramatic moments than an episode of *Eastenders*. From bankruptcy and shock sackings to a Wembley appearance and several big-name signings, supporters had seen it all. But even the most battle-hardened fan had been shaken by this latest twist in the tale.

It was not so much the demise of the Broncos' name and colours that rankled, although that certainly hurt, instead what grated most was that the club's heritage, what little there was of it, had been sacrificed in favour of a partnership – the word 'merger' was banned - with a rugby union club. Not to put too fine a point on it, many league fans viewed union with utter contempt, bitter at the way it had tried to stifle league's popularity since the two codes had gone their separate ways in 1895. As one Broncos fan, perhaps a little insensitively, put it: "Trying to forgive rugby union for trying to strangle the life out of rugby league for more than 100 years is like trying to forgive the Germans and Japanese after World War Two. These people have not given us the time of day in the past and caricatured us as northerners with flat caps and ferrets."

To rub salt into the wounds of those fans smarting from what they considered was an act of betrayal, the club that the Broncos had chosen to link arms with was NEC Harlequins, an institution that many league fans felt represented the very worst union had to offer. It was, in their humble opinion, both a snobbish and pretentious establishment, the very antithesis of everything rugby league stood for.

Not everyone felt so strongly. Some Broncos supporters had long since forgiven rugby union for its indiscretions. Others were simply not bothered by what had happened in the past. Several even stood up for NEC Harlequins, claiming it was no longer the arrogant face of rugby union but a wonderful family club with a heritage that should be treasured not denounced. In fact, the general consensus seemed to be that the partnership threw up more pros than it did cons. There were some Broncos fans who would take some winning over, those that were afraid this latest initiative was just more pie in the sky, but their fears were understandable. After all, the club had witnessed many false dawns since its formation in the autumn of 1980.

For a start, there had been three name changes. The club had started life as Fulham in September 1980 before becoming London Crusaders in 1991 and then London Broncos in 1994. Now it was Harlequins RL, though for how long no one was entirely sure. There had also been, for various lengths of time, a staggering 10 different home venues in the capital. There had been the more permanent residences at Craven Cottage, the National Sports Centre at Crystal Palace, the Polytechnic Stadium in Chiswick, Barnet Copthall Stadium, The Valley, The Stoop and Griffin Park. But the club had also played some games at Stamford Bridge, Wealdstone and Hendon as well as such far-flung places as Leicester, Bridgend and Perpignan. It was an amazing odyssey, but one that had inevitably put deep feelings of insecurity into the minds of some fans who felt the club would never find a place it could really call home.

The majority of Broncos supporters seemed to believe the partnership with NEC Harlequins, which was to last for an initial five years, had real potential. Not only did it provide them with a new home – and one with superb facilities for fans and players alike – it also gave them a certain degree of autonomy. The agreement stipulated that the rugby league club would remain an independent body and would, among other things, receive all the proceeds it generated on match-days. The alliance was more about pooling resources than anything else – and the Broncos had more to gain in that respect. After all, their infrastructure was far inferior to that of NEC Harlequins.

Ian Lenagan's arrival as chairman and joint owner of Harlequins RL was another major plus for a club which had lurched from one financial crisis to another during its 26-year existence. The Wigan-born rugby league devotee possessed not only a multi-million-pound fortune but also a considerable chunk of business and marketing acumen. By deciding to invest in the club, becoming joint owner alongside David Hughes, he had made it clear that he thought it had a big future. That his arrival coincided with the link-up with NEC Harlequins was exactly that, a coincidence. But the double development was hugely significant nonetheless. Fans of the Broncos had more reason than ever to be optimistic.

As Harlequins RL shaped up for the start of the 2006 season, the signs were promising. Ticket sales were up, there were more companies showing an interest in sponsoring the club, and the players were relishing both their new environment and the challenge that lay ahead. What's more, it looked like there would be a big crowd inside the Twickenham Stoop for the club's very first competitive game. Lenagan was certainly confident of a big turnout. The day before the match with St Helens, having invited us up to his Milton Keynes office, he estimated that at least 7,000 spectators would come through the turnstiles. That would represent a hugely positive start.

St Helens were always likely to bring a large following to west London for their first league game of 2006. But few can have expected to witness such a sea of red and white converging on the Stoop. It must have been a sweet sight for Lenagan and Harlequins RL chief executive Nic Cartwright. They were no doubt anxious to see how their team fared out on the pitch, but they could have been forgiven for taking a moment to think about all the attendance money flooding in from the crowd of 8,213.

Inside the ground, the atmosphere was extremely jovial and upbeat. Both sets of supporters were looking forward to the game and were more than happy to share their hopes and fears for the year ahead as they mingled happily in the stands and the concourses. But it was the Harlequins RL fans that attracted most of the attention from the television camera crews that had gathered at the North Stand end of the ground. Keen to record the thoughts of the home spectators before the start of a new season, reporters from Sky and the BBC queued up to speak to them as they came through the turnstiles. By and large, the camera lenses captured smiling faces, the euphoria that accompanies the start of every season eradicating any negative thoughts the Harlequins RL supporters may have had on such an historic day.

One man who shared the optimism of the majority of home fans was rugby league commentator Ray French. A former dual code international, French was at the Stoop to commentate on the game for BBC Radio Merseyside. He was full of enthusiasm for the Harlequins venture and felt those who opposed it were "living in the Dark Ages". However, he sounded one note of caution. If rugby league could not make a go of it at The Stoop, then it was doubtful it would succeed anywhere in the capital.

Like French, Rea certainly hoped this was the start of something big. But he knew that success on the pitch was paramount. If the club was a flop on the field, then nothing else mattered. The Australian had begun preparing for the club's debut season as Harlequins RL long before the players reported back for pre-season training on 24 November 2005. But it was only when he had his hands on the players again that the hard work could really start. The coaching team, which remained largely unchanged from the previous year, immediately began calculating how much fitness the players had lost during the off-season. There were the usual bleep tests, which measure stamina and are greeted with little enthusiasm by the players. Then there were the power sessions in the gym, which gave the beefier boys in the squad the chance to show off their strength.

It was to be a gruelling schedule, but it was not all sweat and toil. The players also got to try on their new Harlequins RL training kit for the first time. For Rea, it was a symbolic moment. Some members of the squad had felt guilty about the demise of the Broncos, wondering whether it was somehow their fault. Rea assured them it was not. Instead, he urged them to look back fondly on their time with the Broncos and insisted the Broncos name should not become taboo. At the same time, he wanted them to embrace the future and take pride in their new identity. He had already said goodbye to the Broncos by donating some of his shirts and programmes to his local charity shop.

With everything that was happening off the pitch and all the changes that had come with the move to the Stoop, Rea recognised it was a challenging time for his players. However, he was not about to tolerate a drop in standards. He had a well-balanced and talented squad at his disposal, boasting such gifted ball-players as Mark McLinden, Luke Dorn and Thomas Leuluai as well as a combative set of forwards that included Danny Williams, Rob Purdham and Lee Hopkins. But after the achievements of 2005, when the club had reached the play-offs and won admirers for its attacking flair, Rea felt his players were not living up to his expectations in the opening weeks of pre-season.

Rea prides himself on producing teams that display grit, heart and unity in abundance, but he felt his squad were failing to do the little things right, the things that had made them successful in the past and ensured that the Broncos had constantly punched above their weight. He was concerned that some members of the squad were cutting corners, arriving for training at the last minute and then cheating themselves and their team-mates when the sessions began by not pushing themselves to the limit. Realising he had to act sooner rather than later for fear of the indiscipline escalating, Rea pulled a couple of them aside and told them that they were selling themselves short. In his words, they were "going to get bitten on the bum" if they did not shape up.

Thankfully, the players heeded the coach's warning and showed a marked change in attitude in the week leading up to the Christmas break. When they returned after the festive season, they impressed their coach still further with their attention to detail. For Rea, it was a real breakthrough. He felt the team had demonstrated a maturity that would stand them in good stead going into another tough and testing Super League campaign.

Harlequins RL continued their pre-season build-up in Perpignan, a destination the club knew well. It was a deliberate move. With so many changes going on around the players, Rea understood the need for some stability. However, not everyone was enamoured with another trip to southern France. Paul Sykes, for one, was not relishing another fortnight of Gallic fare. He had had his fill of baguettes the previous year and could not stomach the thought of being forced to tuck into another one.

Dietary concerns aside, the trip was vital for team bonding. Unlike previous seasons, there had not been a massive turnover of players in the off-season, yet it was important the new signings – the likes of Matt Gafa and Chad Randall - were made to feel at home as quickly as possible. To help the settling-in process and prevent any cliques from forming during the camp, the players were told to swap bedrooms every night so that they ended up sharing with several team-mates during the course of the two weeks. There were the usual card games, too, as well as some more unusual pastimes, like seeing which player could walk fastest in deep snow. Thibault Giroud, the team's new elite performance manager, also used some of his local knowledge to find them a decent nightclub one Friday night.

It was not all rest and relaxation. There was plenty of hard work, too. During the first week, the players were out of bed most days at 6.45am and on the team bus 45 minutes later. After a weights session in the gym, they would grab a bite to eat before the main training session of the day. Lunch followed and then a run on most afternoons, while some time was also set aside for talking tactics.

The whole camp had been planned in advance, much of it by assistant coach Rohan Smith and team manager Dom Fenton. It had to be. Regulations stipulate that the Rugby Football League must be informed when and where clubs are training so drug tests can be carried out. A few years ago, the testers even turned up at a pre-season training camp in Dubai.

Harlequins RL played a low-key match against Leigh while they were in Perpignan and ended their French sojourn with a game against Catalans Dragons. Nic Cartwright flew over for the 46-6 win over the Super League newcomers at the Stade Municipal St Esteve. It was an encouraging display, though it came against a side still in its formative stages and without the services of Stacey Jones, the New Zealand international scrum-half. Still, it was a first win in Quins colours for Rea's side.

Quins left for France without their match kit because it had not arrived from the manufacturers. When it finally turned up in Perpignan, concern was etched all over the face of kitman Steve Magee. On first glance, he felt the shirts were too small. The players had been measured three months previously and he felt that maybe someone had got their figures wrong. Rea summoned four of his squad into his hotel room and watched as they tried on the new shirts, curious not only to find out whether they were the correct size but also to see how the players reacted to the new colours. It turned out that Magee's eyes had deceived him because the jerseys were a perfect fit. What's more, the players loved the pastel quarters. Within 30 minutes, the entire squad had tried everything on. The new kit had received a resounding thumbs-up.

When the squad returned to England in late January, pre-season preparations continued with a friendly against Leeds Rhinos at Headingley. It was a good test. Quins led 18-16 after an hour before eventually going down 28-18 to the 2005 Grand Finalists. Rea was pleased with the workout, but he began to worry about the players' focus as the game against St Helens drew ever nearer. Media attention had increased dramatically as newspapers and broadcasters queued up for a piece of what was clearly a great story. The Broncos upping sticks again and joining forces with one of the bastions of the union game was a unique tale. Throw a mouth-watering clash with Saints into the mix and it was easy to see why Harlequins RL had become such a hot topic.

Just before kick-off against St Helens, Chris Warren, Harlequins RL's marketing and media manager, announced over the tannoy that the Harlequins Hearts would soon be going through their first routine. The Hearts, who might have been the Harlequeens or Jesters had the vote to name them thrown up another result, had replaced the popular Cowgirls as the club's new dance team.

For Lenagan, the pre-match entertainment was almost as important as the action served up on the pitch. Earlier in the week, he had approved a slightly higher spend than had initially been budgeted for to ensure that the match-day experience was much more than just 80 minutes of rugby. That went for every home game, too, not just the opening weekend of the new season. As a consequence, the Hearts were made to share the spotlight on that Saturday afternoon with members of the armed forces, in particular the Royal Marines. As well as wandering around the ground handing out leaflets to potential new recruits, two of their unit abseiled down from the roof of the Lexus Stand with the match ball. Blink and you missed it, but it added to the sense of occasion.

As people started to take their seats and the players took to the field, the Hearts continued to go through their paces. It seemed a bitterly cold day for such a minimal amount of clothing. Their outfits, particularly the skimpy shorts, certainly raised a few eyebrows and generated plenty of opinion.

With just a few minutes to go before kick-off, there were large numbers of fans still trying to locate their seats. But, a few teething troubles aside, it was a world away from the cramped and limited possibilities inside Griffin Park, the club's previous home.

The pre-match entertainment complete, all eyes turned to the players as they marched onto the pitch. This was the moment everyone had been waiting for. St Helens fans expected victory for their side. Harlequins RL fans just crossed their fingers and hoped.

Only a few minutes had elapsed when Rea realised his worst fears were about to come true. Given all the hoo-ha that had accompanied their very first game as Quins, he had worried that his players might not be totally focused on the task at hand. They started well, putting the visitors under some early pressure, but Rea felt they were making too many handling errors. Sure enough, Quins failed to capitalise on their positive opening and Saints scored from their first attacking move, debutant Cayless crossing after seven minutes.

Quins hit back with a Tyrone Smith try that was converted by Gafa, the score prompting Lenagan to dance a jig of delight from his position high in the East Stand. But it was a rare moment of joy for the new chairman. Saints overwhelmed their hosts, with Great Britain full-back Wellens touching down twice in quick succession as Anderson's team took a 24-6 lead into the break.

Harlequins RL had not been helped by the loss of on-field skipper McLinden just minutes before kick-off. The inspirational Australian had pulled a hamstring in training just 24 hours before the game and failed a subsequent fitness test in the warm-up. Instead of leading his side out on such a prestigious day, he spent the afternoon slumped in his seat in the Lexus Stand. He cut a very dejected figure and looked increasingly glum as the day wore on.

Neil Budworth was also stuck in the stands, but his demeanour was altogether more upbeat. The 24-year-old hooker had spent a year on the sidelines after suffering a serious knee injury at the start of the 2005 season. It had been a very lonely existence for the young Wiganer, made worse when his recovery was put back several weeks after his knee became infected. The setback had forced him to dig deep into his reserves of mental strength to ensure he did not crumble, but now his exile was almost at an end after a year of misery and frustration.

Neither Budworth nor McLinden featured in the thoughts of Rea on that second Saturday in February, though. They had ceased to exist, albeit temporarily, as far as the coach was concerned. Rea's philosophy is simple. Only the 17 players in the squad can affect what happens on match-day. Those in the stands are irrelevant.

With McLinden ruled out, Rea had handed the captaincy for the Saints game to Danny Williams, a powerful second-rower and an Australian Grand Final winner with Melbourne Storm in 1999. Rea had also been forced to make a couple of positional changes as a result of McLinden's absence, but he insisted later that these last-minute disruptions were no excuse for his side's first-half performance. In his view, Quins had made it easy for the visitors by turning the ball over far too frequently.

Quins improved after the interval, scoring twice through winger Rikki Sheriffe, a recent recruit from National League side Halifax, and centre Sykes, making an earlier-than-expected return to action following knee surgery. In truth, though, Saints should have taken their points tally past the 50 mark, making break after break as they capitalised on a string of handling errors from Rea's team. It was only their rustiness that denied them a more handsome victory. As for the Quins players, disappointment was etched on all their faces when the final hooter sounded.

Discussion was frank and honest in the Harlequins RL changing room after the game. Set completion was a huge issue for Rea, who felt his team had fallen well short of their targets. The large number of individual errors bewildered him, too. The coach also felt his team had been far too quiet on the pitch and communication had been poor as a result. Budworth had commented during the game that the players had been nervous, perhaps caught up in the significance of the day. It was a sentiment that was echoed by club skipper Purdham, who admitted he had never felt so on edge before a game of rugby league, and Hopkins, who felt the players had been caught up in all the hysteria that had surrounded the move to the Stoop. "There was an air of expectancy for the first game against St Helens," said Hopkins. "It was a big occasion and maybe got to a few people. We were hearing how well the club was doing off the field, getting constant updates about how well ticket sales were going. In retrospect, it might have been better to let us concentrate on training and playing."

Rea's demeanour in the post-match press conference said it all. Anderson had faced the media first and seemed surprisingly flat given his side had run in seven tries, three of them from Wellens. The St Helens coach said his team had been "scratchy" and dropped too much ball.

If Anderson was downbeat, Rea had the look of a man who would rather be anywhere else than in front of the press. He emanated a sense of crushing disappointment and would, days later, admit that facing the media that Saturday afternoon had been a chastening experience.

Lenagan mingled with supporters in the King's Bar as Rea tried to come to terms with the loss. The chairman was evidently disappointed with the result but delighted with the day. He had every right to be pleased. A crowd of 8,213 had watched the match, a figure above even the most optimistic estimates.

Mark Evans, NEC Harlequins' chief executive, shared Lenagan's optimism. St Helens may have left with the points but he felt the big winners had been Harlequins. Asked whether he felt a heavy defeat in front of a sizeable crowd was more important than a close contest played out in a half-empty stadium, he eventually conceded it was more important, at this juncture, to get as many people through the turnstiles. In his view, exposing rugby league to a wider public was vital and this was just one reverse. Quins had another 27 league games to put things right on the field.

Back in the King's Bar, fans of both Harlequins RL and St Helens mixed easily. The post-match entertainment was in full flow while, to the delight of Saints fans, Wigan's shock defeat by Super League newcomers Catalans was being shown live on the big screen.

The Quins players eventually appeared, and the dreadlocked Karl Temata was named the home side's man of the match thanks to his athletic and combative display. The former New Zealand Warriors forward, who had arrived in London at the tail end of the 2005 season, proved to be a man of few words, leaving acting skipper Williams to thank the fans for their support.

Their duties complete, the players made a beeline for one of the back rooms when the signal came for them to tuck into their post-match meal. Making his way through the bar, Sykes, who had come on as a second-half substitute, said his lack of match fitness had hampered his effectiveness. At one point during the game, he said his lungs felt like they were burning. No doubt he would have liked a couple of days to recover from his exertions. But, eager to put their disappointment behind them, the players decided they would train the following morning.

While his players went home to soothe their battered egos and aching bodies, Rea went out for a meal with friends in an attempt to take his mind of rugby league for a few hours. Some coaches like to start their analysis of a match straight after it has finished. Rea doesn't. He prefers to clear his mind and then begin work again with a fresh perspective.

However, if he thought he was going to get time to refocus, he was sadly mistaken. As he ate his meal at a local steak house, his dining buddies grilled him about the match. Rea asked them politely to change the subject, but his appeal fell on stony ground. As he was forced to digest the loss to Saints as well as his food, he can only have hoped that the Stoop would prove more fertile territory in the coming months.

Win, lose or draw, 11 February 2006 marked the dawning of yet another new era for rugby league in London. This time, though, there was real belief that the club had left the bad times behind it. Financially, it appeared rock-solid, while the Stoop provided it with a home that any Super League club would have been proud to call its own. The key now was success on the pitch – and that was down to the coaching staff and the players. For the fans, it was a case of watching and hoping.

Smile please! The team line up for the cameras,
full of hope for the 2006 season.
(Photos: Philip Gordos)

2. Keeping the faith

"It was hard to motivate staff to sell another 10 tickets worth £150 when we were losing £1.5 million a year. We were busting our balls to stay afloat. It was a lot of pain for a few people to take."
Nic Cartwright, Harlequins RL chief executive

Mike Wreford was emotionally drained but deliriously happy. He had just watched his Harlequins RL team claim an unexpected point against Bradford, ending the Bulls' run of 14 successive wins in the process. What's more, the draw had come at Odsal, a ground that had witnessed numerous demolitions of visiting teams.

Odsal is an unusual venue. Built in a valley, it is well camouflaged from the street and easy to miss if you have not been before. Inside, it is both spectacular and inspiring. Enter the ground through the turnstiles on Rooley Avenue and your eyes are immediately drawn to the pitch laid out below you. Though not quite Narnia at the back of your wardrobe, it is an impressive sight. Standing at this end of the stadium, on the big blocks of concrete that form the terracing, it is easy to see why Odsal is often described as a natural amphitheatre. Supporters get to look down on the action in much the same way as bloodthirsty spectators would have gazed down on the gladiatorial combats of Roman times. The venue possesses none of the grandeur of the Colosseum in Rome – in truth it is a mish-mash of buildings and a little shabby round the edges - but it has earned praise for its atmosphere on match-days. Even opposition players like running out here.

Mike had arrived at the ground 90 minutes before the 6pm kick-off for the Super League game between Bradford and Harlequins RL in order to meet fellow Quins supporters Percy Pettifor and Emily Toplis outside the ground. They were not hard to miss. It wasn't the pastel-quartered replica shirts that marked them out but their garish yellow shorts covered in Quins red and blue diamond shapes. It had been a lovely day in West Yorkshire, but their attire soon drew a string of disbelieving looks from the locals.

When Mike, Percy and Emily walked through the turnstiles to take up a spot on the terraces, there was already a game going on. Harlequins RL's newly reformed Senior Academy side was in action against Bradford – and getting a real battering. Already fearing a thumping for the first team, the sight of the under-21s being cut to ribbons in a 62-10 defeat did not bode well. The Bulls may have been without Great Britain skipper Jamie Peacock, who had signed for Leeds in the off-season, while inspirational winger Lesley Vainikolo was sidelined by injury, but the Super League champions still possessed world-class players in Stuart Fielden, recognised as one of the best props in the game, and centre Shontayne Hape, who had helped New Zealand pull off a shock win in the Gillette Tri-Nations Series at the end of 2005. They had recently added the World Club Challenge trophy to their growing list of honours, too.

Despite their sense of foreboding, Mike, Percy and Emily had not thought twice about making the trip to Odsal. For Mike, the journey from Staines on the outskirts of west London covered around 200 miles and lasted four hours. For Percy and Emily, it was a relatively short trip across the Pennines from their home in the coastal town of Morecambe, just west of Lancaster.

Percy and Emily have not always lived in Morecambe, but then they hadn't spent much time in London either. Born and brought up in Yorkshire – Percy is from Halifax while Emily hails from Doncaster - they started supporting London when they were living in Bedford, a round-trip of around 120 miles, and continued to follow the club when they headed to the Cumbrian coast. The couple have racked up thousands and thousands of miles supporting the club. In 2005 they travelled more than 10,000 miles to cheer their team on. Make that around 12,000 if you include the flight to the south of France for the 'On-the-road' game against Leeds in Perpignan. Just quite how much their devotion costs them in cold, hard cash is not something they are willing to contemplate. Perhaps finding out would jolt them so hard it would make them question their loyalty.

The news got worse for the three as they waited for the main event to begin. Not only had they witnessed the final stages of the Senior Academy's humbling, they had discovered that Luke Dorn had joined Mark McLinden and Tyrone Smith on the sidelines, along with long-term casualties Chad Randall, Neil Budworth and Tim Hartley. The absence of Dorn, the former Northern Eagles and Sydney Roosters half-back, came as a big blow. One of the club's most talented individuals, his form in pre-season, especially the game against Leeds at Headingley, suggested this would be another sparking year for the 23-year-old Australian. Supporters were salivating at the prospect of seeing Dorn, McLinden and the equally mercurial Thomas Leuluai - or the 'Golden Triangle' as they were referred to by some fans - rip opposing defences to shreds with their darting runs and dazzling ball skills.

The three fans chose not to ruminate too much on the loss of Dorn and the selection posers facing coach Tony Rea. More important for them was their choice of chant. Since the club had adopted the Harlequins name, the overhaul of their choral repertoire had taken place in earnest. Some tunes, like 'Tony Rea's Barmy Army', required no tinkering at all. But they were still after something fresh, a chant that would symbolise their loyalty to the new cause. One of the early favourites was 'We're smart, we're cute, our shirt looks just like puke, Harlequins, Harlequins!' It may not have captured the dawning of a new era, but such self-deprecating humour went down a storm with the Bradford fans.

Not so popular with the home supporters was the Bulls' performance. When hooker Ian Henderson cut through the Harlequins RL defence after just eight minutes, it looked as though the visiting fans had been right to be full of trepidation ahead of the game. But as the match wore on, it became clear Quins were not going to crumble. Quite the opposite, in fact. Sensing all was not well, it was the home fans who became increasingly restless.

Forced to promote Tony Clubb, a hugely promising but still green winger, to their 17-man squad because of mounting injuries, the Quins began to get the measure of their hosts. By half-time, they were 12-6 up thanks to tries from Leuluai and Danny Williams, with Paul Sykes converting both scores. The Bulls hit back straight after the break, tries from Hape and Ben Harris giving them a 16-12 lead. But again Quins refused to buckle, their defence more than standing up to the home side's pressure. They were even able to exert some of their own. When Lee Hopkins scythed his way through the Bulls defence to touch down under the posts on the hour mark, the unthinkable became thinkable.

The Bradford fans grew more and more frustrated, upset with their own side's lack of poise but also turning up their criticism of referee Ashley Klein, who was not enjoying the most productive of days. He had made several controversial calls, upsetting both Rea and opposite number Brian Noble. But it was the Bulls who were handed a lifeline they scarcely deserved as the visitors looked set for a famous win.

Paul Deacon, playing only his third competitive game since suffering a life-threatening facial injury while on Tri-Nations duty for Great Britain in 2005, had already missed one chance to kick Bradford level when Williams, captain again in McLinden's absence, was penalised for obstruction. The penalty should have gone to the visitors for Hape's incorrect play-the-ball moments before, but Deacon was not about to spurn another opportunity to salvage a point. His kick sailed between the sticks to tie the scores at 18-18. Quins made one last desperate bid to snatch victory, but Sykes was off target with an ambitious drop-goal attempt.

Rea felt Quins had been robbed of victory and made his feelings clear to the media after the game. Despite his disappointment, he still applauded the small group of Quins fans who had stayed on to cheer his team off the pitch. The players, clearly weary from the enormous efforts, clapped the supporters, too, before heading for a well-earned shower and feed.

Sykes admitted later he had been left drained by his exertions on the field and thought most of the players would need a few more weeks to get up to speed. "The players feel they still have a lot more work to do," he said. "We are looking to build on the performance. For most of the teams at this time of the season, it takes three or four games to get back into the swing of things."

Quins had got their first point of Super League XI, leaving Mike, Percy and Emily ecstatic. They had journeyed to Bradford full of hope but had expected a defeat. Now they were going home revitalised and in joyous mood. "I've seen us get spanked here before," said Mike, who was feeling the strain of cheering on his team. "My throat is sore, my neck hurts and my heart is pounding away, but it's been worth it. This is what it's all about."

Save for one notable occasion, Odsal had not been a happy hunting ground for London, which made the 18-18 draw on 18 February even more significant. The last time the team had left Bradford in buoyant mood was on 1 June 2003, when the Broncos recorded one of the most extraordinary victories in Super League history. The Bulls went into that game on the back of a 13-match winning streak but walked off the pitch having been beaten 22-12. It was not simply that Bradford had been upset on their own ground by a team scratching around in the middle of the table that the game became part of rugby league folklore. The reason the match attracted so much media attention was Dennis Moran.

The Australian scrum-half had only arrived back in the country a few hours before kick-off after returning home in midweek to attend a family funeral. But Moran, showing no physical ill-effects from the long journey and clearly sharp as a tack mentally, ripped the Bulls to shreds, scoring the first of his three tries that day after four minutes and inspiring the rest of his team to a remarkable success. Noble had been quick to sing Moran's praises. "He was the difference in the end, I thought he was great," enthused the vanquished Bradford coach. "On the evidence of his performance, I think we should send one or two of our players back to Australia for the week."

The latest heroics at Odsal may not have boasted any of the individual brilliance that had lit up the ground in the corresponding fixture three seasons ago, but it was arguably just as significant. At least, that was the view of Percy. He reckoned that, because Sky Sports had screened the game live, the damage done by the feeble loss to St Helens the week before had largely been eradicated.

Percy was in a mood to celebrate. So were Emily and Mike. After accepting congratulations from some Bradford fans appreciative of their raucous support, they celebrated their side's gutsy showing with a meal at a Little Chef, just a stone's throw from Odsal. There, the banter with the locals continued. One waitress, after confessing to being a Bradford fan, came in for some gentle goading which she took in her stride.

While they waited for their food to arrive, Percy, Emily and Mike reflected on the changes to their club. They were hopeful it was moving in the right direction, confident that the link-up with NEC Harlequins would finally give it the stability they craved. They accepted that not every fan was totally committed to the new venture but felt the dissenters would come round in time once they had finished their self-imposed period of mourning for the Broncos and overcome whatever fears or concerns they had of forging a relationship with one of the bastions of rugby union. They were also confident the atmosphere would eventually improve at home matches. The Saints game was clear evidence that the change in identity had unsettled many supporters. "People were confused," said Mike. "They didn't know what to chant." Percy was candid enough to admit that he still made the mistake of shouting for London rather Harlequins RL but saw no harm in "learning on the job". "Shouting for Quins is a habit people will have to get into," he added, predicting it could take until next season for the atmosphere to warm up at the Stoop.

Fans of London's top-flight rugby league club have had to put up with a string of major upheavals since its inception 26 years ago. Given the number of financial crises that have gripped the club at various stages in its short but colourful history, it's fair to say that it's never been a smooth ride for supporters. Dave Fiddler, a Warrington fan who switched his allegiance to London after moving south, sums up most fans' views about the club's precarious past when he says: "You never quite knew whether the club was going to be around the following season."

Supporters have gone to extreme lengths to ensure London survived the many threats to its future. Barry Warren was among a group of fans that helped carry the goalposts along the banks of the River Thames from Craven Cottage in Fulham to Chiswick when the Polytechnic Stadium became the club's new home in 1985. "It took half a day to complete the journey," he recalled. He also helped paint the ramshackle pavilion and clear the terraces of weeds, rubble and goodness knows what else in order to make the place hospitable.

There are numerous other examples of London fans going out of their way to keep the club afloat. Their acts of loyalty would fill a whole book. But they also spend a lot of time, effort and hard-earned cash simply turning up to watch the team each weekend.

As anyone who lives in or has visited London will tell you, making your way around the capital is not a straightforward affair. It can take anything from an hour to two hours to get from one side of the city to the other, even when the transport system is running smoothly. When there are problems with the roads, trains or London Underground – and hardly a day goes by when there isn't some kind of breakdown – the travelling time can quickly double. Factor in an away trip every other week – the shortest journey for London-based Harlequins RL fans in Super League XI was the 380-mile round-trip to Wakefield - and you get some idea of the lengths the club's followers go to just to cheer on their team.

Ask Emily if the devotion of the club's fans sets them apart from supporters at, say, Widnes, Castleford or Hull and her reply is emphatic. "We are no more dedicated or loyal than other fans," she told us. But not everyone agrees. Rob Purdham, Harlequins RL's club captain for 2006, thinks supporters in London put up with more than most. "They are the most loyal fans in the game," he insisted. It is a sentiment echoed by former Broncos player Tulsen Tollett. "No matter how small the group is, you are always aware of them," said the Broncos legend, who now commentates on rugby league for both Sky and the BBC. "They are a hardy bunch and I always made a point of thanking them after a game."

London fans regularly come under fire from their counterparts in the north. Ignorance plays its part, as does jealousy and a sense that London receives more than its fair share of favours from the rugby league hierarchy. One of those 'favours' concerns the overseas quota system. Other Super League clubs, apart from 2006 newcomers Catalans Dragons, are allowed just three overseas players in their squads. But Harlequins RL, like the Broncos before them, for the 2006 season were limited to five. Not that other clubs have been prevented from packing their sides full of players from outside Great Britain. Exploitation of United Kingdom residency regulations and the controversial Kolpak ruling, which until the end of the 2006 season allowed players from countries that have an associate agreement with the European Union the same rights as a European, means the likes of Bradford have been able to hoover up talent from abroad. Against the Harlequins, the Bulls fielded just eight players who qualify to play for the Lions.

Yet it is Quins who are criticised for their perceived over-reliance on players from the southern hemisphere and their inability to attract personnel from the north of England. London fan Brian Pollard recalled one away trip to Castleford Tigers. "When our team ran out, they played the *Neighbours* theme tune," he said. "We always get the mickey taken out of us, saying we are a team full of Aussies." Tollett, whose Australian accent belies the fact that he toured with Great Britain, says the mickey-taking is to be expected. "We were always classed as an Australian team when I played," he said. "To a certain extent we still are. Thirteen of the 17 players in the Saints game were from Down Under."

Many London supporters enjoy the banter with their rival fans, but is the flak that comes their way indicative of a deeper feeling of antagonism towards rugby league in the capital? Several think it is. "Some clubs just don't want to have anything to do with those outside the M62 corridor," said Michael Waite, a Yorkshireman by birth but now very much a fan of London. "They think we are either Cockney gits or Aussies." David Mace, who has been a supporter of London since the first game against Wigan in 1980, added: "We go up north and the fans there still think we don't know anything about rugby league. They think we are a charity case, always getting favours."

Comments made by Peter Roe prior to the start of the season appeared to support the view that there are those in the game who think rugby league in London is a waste of time and effort. In an article in *The Guardian*, Roe, who can list Wakefield, Featherstone, Barrow, Swinton and Halifax among the list of clubs he has coached, said he would love rugby league to increase in popularity across the United Kingdom. However, he felt London was infertile ground. "I just don't think rugby league will ever be a goer in London, wherever it's played - and they've tried enough different grounds already," he wrote. "There are too many obstacles, too many other things for people to do."

Roe has a point. With 13 major football clubs – Chelsea, Arsenal, Tottenham, West Ham, Charlton, Fulham, Watford, Crystal Palace, Millwall, QPR, Brentford, Leyton Orient and Barnet – and several established rugby union clubs in and around London, rugby league has its work cut out establishing itself in the capital. As Mace concedes, the game does not have the same standing as either football or rugby union. "We have always struggled to gain acceptance," he said. "Lots of people in London used to ask me all the time what the Broncos were. Was it a baseball or an American football team?" His wife, Janet, agrees. "We have always been the poor relations and never been taken seriously, she said. "The view has been that it's a hobby for whoever has owned the club. My friends at work still think I am crazy for being a rugby league fan and following the club everywhere."

Roe's views may or may not be typical of a lot of rugby league fans, but they deserve closer scrutiny. Coach of Keighley at the time of writing, his criticism of London was somewhat expected.

After all, it was Keighley who were controversially - and some would say cruelly - overlooked when Super League was formed in 1995. The Cougars looked to have booked their place in the new competition by winning promotion from the old Second Division only to be told that London, who finished second behind them, were being admitted to Super League instead. In Roe's eyes, the move was not only an act of betrayal; it was another example of London getting a favour they hardly deserved.

As biased as his opinion may be, Roe raises several important questions. Should London have a top-flight rugby league club? More importantly, does it deserve one? Ian Lenagan, the chairman and joint owner of Harlequins RL, believes it does and is quick to defend the club's continued existence in the highest echelon of British rugby league. He admits the numerous ground moves and lack of silverware has undermined its bid for acceptance as a major player, but he leaves no one in any doubt that the future, in his opinion, is bright. He made that plain in the same *Guardian* article that Roe made his critical remarks.

But there are still plenty of people who argue that expanding the game into areas where it is not traditionally strong will only harm the overall product. Paul Coward, a season-ticket holder at Leeds Rhinos and website manager of www.southstander.com, says there has to be some justification for pursuing London as a Super League franchise. So far, he feels, the evidence is pretty flimsy. "If the game was going to get more coverage in the national press as a result, then people would recognise the importance of having a big rugby league club in London, but that doesn't seem to have happened," he said. Damningly, he believes the London club still has not convinced enough people that it is serious about the game. "It is still a novelty club," he added. "My heart says rugby league will grow in strength in London because it's a better game than union and should have more appeal to the advertisers and television people. But my head says that it is not viable as a long-term proposition."

More than 25 years on from its formation, London still needs plenty of friends as it seeks to convince the doubters that it deserves to be taken seriously. It found out just how many friends it has among the Super League fraternity on 4 March 2005. Representatives of all 12 top-flight clubs, plus Richard Lewis and Nigel Wood, the Rugby Football League's executive chairman and finance director respectively, gathered in one of the conference rooms at Huddersfield's Galpharm Stadium to decide whether the Broncos should be kicked out of the league after going into liquidation with debts of £3 million.

"I remember that Friday afternoon vividly," said London fan Ron Knox. "I was permanently watching the news streams and message boards for information. I didn't know what to expect. I was always optimistic but I was a nervous wreck." Not everyone fretted as much as Ron, but the future of the Broncos did indeed hang by a thread as critics turned up the heat. Leading the calls for London to be wiped off the Super League map was then Bradford Bulls chairman Chris Caisley. He argued that the club had to pay some price for its inability to look after its finances.

After a four-and-a-half hour meeting, a vote was called. Broncos chairman David Hughes and chief executive Nic Cartwright had done their best to convince the doubters that London deserved another chance. In fact, so desperate had they been to win support that they had almost let slip the fact the club was planning to join forces with NEC Harlequins by the end of the year. Work on the historic link-up had been going on for months and was close to fruition, but it was still top secret. News of the partnership would only be made public six months later.

For London, fighting for its very existence was nothing new. The club was in a similar predicament in 2001, when it became homeless again after being asked to leave The Valley by Charlton FC, who could no longer accommodate rugby league. Talk of a merger with Leigh and other possible moves away from the capital surfaced. However, and somewhat ironically, it was Caisley, the man who would call for London's extinction four years later, who led the pleas for clemency. With Super League still recovering from the demise of Paris St Germain and Gateshead Thunder, Caisley, who was then Super League chairman, felt the loss of another team would be a major blow to the competition's credibility.

The Broncos were eventually thrown another lifeline, moving to Griffin Park, the home of Brentford FC. But the club continued to haemorrhage cash. Cartwright, who had joined the club as a temporary accountant in 1998 only to become chief executive just three years later, did his best to keep it viable. But even with the support of the Rugby Football League and Broncos chairman Hughes, who was pumping in an estimated £1 million of his own money each year, it was a tough task.

"It was hard to motivate staff to sell another 10 tickets worth £150 when we were losing £1.5 million a year," revealed Cartwright, who says that there was never a moment when he was not acutely aware of the club's precarious financial position. "We were busting our balls to stay afloat. It was a lot of pain for a few people to take."

Despite all the bad times, Cartwright never once thought of quitting the club. "You get too attached," he told us. He also revealed that the challenge of making a success of Super League in the capital was a big reason for him staying put.

But Cartwright's loyalty has come at a price. He says he sacrificed his original career in order to make the club viable. He had been an accountant with Sainsbury's, Ernst & Young and Phillip Morris in Australia at one time or another before joining the Broncos. "I had a career path mapped out for me before I came to the club. Now I haven't got one," he said.

The move to Brentford in 2001 safeguarded London's immediate future but its financial status continued to be a major source of concern. With average attendances for Super League matches at Griffin Park hovering around the 3,500 mark, the term "self-supporting" could not be applied to the club. "You didn't have to be Einstein to work out the figures didn't stack up," said Tollett, whose five-year stint at the club spanned the move to and from The Valley. "When you knew what the players were getting and saw the attendances, it wasn't hard to work out it couldn't carry on."

Virgin's takeover of the club at the end of 1997 had promised so much but had ultimately proved another false dawn. The club had changed ownership several times since its formation in 1980, surviving one bankruptcy and numerous other scares. But there was a genuine feeling that, with Sir Richard Branson's business acumen on their side, the good times were about to roll. The momentous trip to the Challenge Cup Final in 1999 seemed to justify the faith people had in the new venture. But, behind the scenes, the club continued to slide further into debt. Realising he had backed a loser, Branson eventually sold up to Hughes in September 2001.

Hughes, who was and still is a director of Premiership football club Charlton, is owed a huge debt of gratitude by London fans for the way he dug deep into his own pockets to keep the club afloat, but his stewardship was only papering over the cracks. By March 2005 the financial problems eventually came to a head. A tax bill of £1.5 million constituted the bulk of the £3 million debt and was ultimately the reason the club went under. Hughes and Cartwright had offered to pay the money back in instalments but the Inland Revenue demanded payment in full. Rather than getting something, they got nothing. The club went bankrupt, wiping out its debts in one fell swoop.

London's troubles were far from over. Given just a day's notice, Hughes and Cartwright headed north for the 4 March meeting to try to convince the 11 other Super League clubs and RFL chief Lewis that they were an asset not a liability and should be saved.

According to Cartwright, the emergency meeting proved to be a "bit sticky". It was an understatement if ever there was one.

Almost five hours later, they emerged emotionally drained but very relieved. As expected, Caisley had been the biggest obstacle. He felt London had exhausted its chances, that it was obvious to everyone that the capital could not sustain a major rugby league club. Now, in his view, it was time to pull the plug and give another club the opportunity to play in the top flight. In the run-up to the meeting, rumours were rife that Castleford Tigers, relegated the previous season, had been approached to take the Broncos' place if they were expelled.

Caisley was not the only dissenter, although he was the most vocal. Wigan, Salford and Leigh also felt London had outstayed their welcome. Leigh's opposition did not come as a surprise. The demise of the Broncos would perhaps mean one less club going down at the end of the season. As it turned out, the Centurions finished rock bottom after a dismal campaign that yielded just two wins and one draw. With two sides going down in order to accommodate the new French franchise, Catalans Dragons, not even London's expulsion would have spared Leigh from the drop.

Crucially for the Broncos, they won the support of Leeds, St Helens, Hull, Warrington and Huddersfield. But that still left Wakefield and Widnes. If both joined the Caisley ranks, London were out. In the end, it came down to a simple vote: Should London be booted out of Super League? There had been calls for a points penalty instead, but Hughes and Cartwright felt it was an all-or-nothing case. "Either back us or sack us," was their cry. It was a risky strategy but it worked. Wakefield and Widnes abstained rather than side with Caisley. London survived thanks to a 5-4 vote in their favour.

Cartwright was grateful for the reprieve. "There were enough clubs out there who realised it was worth giving us another opportunity to try to make it work," he said at the time. "We have been open and honest with the RFL from the outset and I would like to thank them and the clubs for their support."

Lewis felt the outcome was the right one too. "The decision was in the best interests of the engage Super League and the difficulties experienced by the London Broncos do not reflect the overall health and success of Super League in general," he insisted. "London Broncos now have an opportunity to enter a new era and become an increasingly successful part of the Super League."

But Caisley was furious. He felt London had escaped scot-free. More than that, they had gained an unfair advantage. He had a case, not only were London allowed to play on, they kept the four points they had already won. "I never cease to be amazed by the goings-on in league," he fumed. "Many businesses face difficulties but we ought not to celebrate when those problems are overcome by simply walking away from them. A club that has left the Inland Revenue with a £1.5 million debt and moved its players to a new debt-free company gets royally applauded in the media for surmounting its financial difficulties. The business is then allowed to freely compete in the Super League competition and to do so without penalty. Bizarrely, not only is the new entrant not penalised, it is given the four competition points which were earned by the old club!"

The new company formed to run London was required to adhere to a number of conditions before being given membership of Super League (Europe) Ltd. But their reprieve still left a sour taste in the mouths of many and only cemented the feeling that the Broncos were a charity case, always getting a leg up.

BBC Sports commentator Dave Woods, who four years earlier had argued that London's cause was a lost one, praised the decision to keep the club alive but felt a dangerous precedent had been set. "There will be those disturbed by the fact that having run up an uncontrollable debt, the Broncos are allowed to simply ditch it and then start all over again with no penalty," he wrote. "Fining the new company that has taken over the running of the club would have been an inappropriate gesture. But docking the new club points would have helped ease the conscience of the game. Clubs have been docked points for overspending on the salary cap, so surely a similar penalty would have been appropriate for a club that has overspent by £3 million in other areas. The governance of the game also needs to be looked into. The fate of the Broncos was decided by the other 11 Super League clubs. Imagine if several of those clubs decided they would vote London out, simply to ensure that they themselves weren't relegated this season. It's that potential for short-term, narrow-visioned thinking that has got the game into so much trouble in the past and needs to be addressed. Thank heavens London Broncos have survived and their future is assured, but let's not think that is an end to the matter."

The RFL promised to tighten up their rules governing overspending in the wake of the Broncos saga. "While London are undoubtedly relieved to have been saved, it cannot be allowed to mask the serious issue raised," said Nigel Wood, the RFL's finance director and chief operating officer. "I expect the RFL to review its rules and make recommendations. Perhaps we can learn something from other sports, particularly as regards the sanctions and penalties that may be available to ensure that defaulting clubs are not seen to have gained a competitive advantage." The RFL was true to its word. But it wasn't until 26 February 2006, almost 12 months later, that it attempted to stop sides gaining advantage by unaffordable overspending. From that date, the RFL decreed that any club becoming insolvent would be docked six points. Had such a penalty been in existence when London were experiencing their travails, they would not have made the play-offs that year.

While Hughes and Cartwright had fought for London's future, the players waited anxiously for news from Huddersfield, having been promised a text message from Rea informing them if the club was still alive. Well, not all of them were anxious. Joe Mbu refused to worry about the meeting. He had complete faith in Cartwright and Hughes, confident they would deliver. "I trust the club to look after me and they trust me to do my job, to look after my body and perform," he told us, 12 months on from that momentous day. "There's no point worrying about things you can't control. What happened was out of my hands. It would have affected my training and playing if I had worried about it."

Not everyone was as calm as Mbu. Rob Purdham admits it was an unsettling time, especially once agents out to profit from London's predicament got wind that the club could fold. For Lee Hopkins, it was not just an unsettling time, it was traumatic. He had been at the club for just a couple of months following his move from NRL side Parramatta Eels when his future was suddenly thrown into the air. But at least there was a possible silver lining. Thinking the Broncos were on the verge of collapse, Wigan made it clear they would like to sign the Sydney-born second-rower. Even after London had survived, the Warriors, coached by Denis Betts, continued their pursuit. "It was three days of hell. I didn't sleep at all," recalled Hopkins, who was torn over his loyalty to the Broncos and the need to safeguard his career. "I wasn't the only player being chased either. The vultures were circling around the whole team." What made the decision-making process more exasperating for the Australian was that Wigan expected him to play against the Broncos on 11 March should he move to the JJB Stadium.

"It was 50:50 whether I would go or stay," admitted Hopkins. "At that point I'd had no assurances about what was going on. I was getting a lot of information second hand and I wasn't sure what to believe. In the end, I decided to do my own research to find out the truth about what was going on. I made phone calls to Australia and spoke to my former coaches and people I respected and trusted. Then, at the 11th hour, I went for lunch with David Hughes, Tony Rea and Mark McLinden in Knightsbridge. David Hughes was unbelievable. He assured me things were fine. That was what I wanted to hear. I wanted to know from the top of the tree that things were fine." After a quick chat with his wife, Rochelle, Hopkins had made his mind up, he knew what he was going to do. To the relief of Hughes, Rea and McLinden, he turned down the move to Wigan. "I had a couple of minutes talking with my wife and that was it, it was sewn up," he said. "I was staying."

The rest of the team also pledged their loyalty to the club after getting the reassurances they were after. "We stood by each other and the club," said Purdham. As if Hopkins needed proof he had made the right choice, London beat Wigan 34-20 at Griffin Park on 11 March and went on to finish above the Warriors in the table.

Rea understands better than most the problems the club has faced and overcome in the past. After ending his playing career and before becoming coach, he had a short spell as the club's chief executive. But even he had an attack of the nerves on the day of the Huddersfield meeting. "There was a period when it was a major concern for a few hours in the afternoon," he recalled. Rea had expected a phone call around midday, but it did not come until much, much later. One o'clock came and went, so did two, then three. Finally at four, when the doubts had really started to take hold, he got the news he wanted. "Fortunately, common sense prevailed," he said.

The players received a text from Rea with the good news, but the fans had to wait a little longer for an announcement on the club's future. "I think I celebrated with a few glasses of champagne with my wife that night. I couldn't imagine my life without the Broncos," recalled Ron Knox. Fellow London supporter Barry Warren, on the other hand, had always anticipated a reprieve. "I took it all with a pinch of salt," he said. "I didn't think we would be kicked out. I've seen it so many times. Something is always pulled out at the eleventh hour."

Purdham says the revelation that four clubs – Bradford, Wigan, Salford and Leigh - had voted to kick London out of Super League only enhanced the feeling amongst a lot of the players that it was "us against the rest". The fans felt the same way. "You get a sort of siege mentality here because of all the problems the club has faced," said Knox, a long-time Warrington supporter before deciding to follow London. "I feel like an evangelist for the game at times. I've got a kind of missionary zeal. People in Warrington take the club for granted because rugby league is part of the community. In London it is totally different."

The good news for London as it attempted to pick up the pieces after the meeting in Huddersfield was that it had already taken a major step towards financial salvation. Cartwright and Hughes had started speaking to a potential backer in February. Both men were hopeful, but it was not until July that a deal was eventually tied up. It was worth the wait. After years of hardship, not knowing if they were going to survive from one season to the next, London had hit the jackpot.

The potential backer turned out to be Ian Lenagan, a self-made businessman worth millions. The Wiganer had been a rugby league fan for 50 years but had shown little interest in putting any of his hard-earned cash into the sport until he was introduced to Hughes. Well, that's not strictly true. He had set up two £1,000-a-year scholarships to help some of the sport's brightest prospects study at Oxford University, but he had not been persuaded to take the big plunge until the plight of the Broncos was brought to his attention. "I had never really thought about getting involved in the business of rugby league," he said. "But, through my work with Oxford University, I met up with a number of people, businessmen and rugby league people, and we talked about businessmen getting involved with the sport. Two and a half months later, when the Broncos hit rocky times, I got a phone call asking if I was serious. That is how it all started for me."

Lenagan, also a successful theatre producer, is not one to take snap decisions. He certainly would not throw his money away on a lost cause. "I thought long and hard about whether to get involved with the Broncos as they were then," he said. Ironically, the proposed link-up with Harlequins, which was on the verge of fruition, made Lenagan think twice before putting his money into the Broncos. "At first I didn't like the idea of changing the name to Harlequins, but when you look at the business aspects of it, it's a no-brainer," he said.

Lenagan agreed to invest in the Broncos on a handshake - "the way David Hughes and I do business" - in an Indian restaurant in central London. However, it was several months before he made his involvement official. He eventually put pen to paper on 22 July 2005, not only becoming joint owner alongside Hughes but also chairman. For Cartwright, it was a significant moment. "This is simply fantastic news for the club," he enthused at the time. "For David to attract a man of Ian's pedigree, enthusiasm and standing says much about our club and about our former chairman. This will allow us to take even further steps forward as a club." Hughes was equally upbeat. "We welcome Ian to the club and I am very excited about working with him to take the club to the next level."

Seven months on from becoming the joint owner of Harlequins RL, Lenagan must have felt he had made the right decision after seeing Quins draw at Bradford. The result was a big shot in the arm and a huge confidence booster for the team going into the home game against Wakefield the following Saturday. McLinden and Dorn, two of the club's most influential players, would miss the match but a win over Wakefield, who had lost to Bradford and Hull in their two opening games, was almost taken for granted, if not by the players then certainly by the fans. Was that why the eventual 26-6 loss hit harder than one of Mike Tyson's uppercuts? Semi Tadulala had the Quins on the ropes with two tries in the first 10 minutes. The 6 feet 2 inches Fijian winger then completed his hat-trick six minutes from time to make the score 26-0. Mark Tookey crossed under the posts late on for the home side but it was scant consolation.

The defeat was a body blow to Quins in more ways than one. Not only did it deprive them of what they anticipated would be their first win, it also put another dent in the club's drive to get more people through the turnstiles. The home defeat to St Helens on the opening weekend had dampened some of the fervour generated by the intense pre-season marketing campaign but was not regarded as disastrous for the club's long-term objectives. But a tame loss at home to the Wildcats, a team that was expected to spend most of the season hovering around the relegation zone, was more serious.

A crowd of 3,554 had witnessed one of the least attractive matches on the fixture calendar. Not a bad turn-out, but how many would return for the next home game against Castleford in a fortnight's time?

Lenagan had spent a lot of time examining attendance figures before Super League XI kicked off. He may have millions at his disposal, but he was - and remains - determined not to allow the club to become a drain on his finances. "One of the basic tenets of any business that I have is that it has to wash its face, it has to break even," he said. "David Hughes had been putting in roughly £1 million a year to prop up the losses and there is a limit to how much of that you can do because it becomes debilitating, you are not going forward."

According to Nic Cartwright, it costs £3 million a year to run a Super League club. Before the 2006 campaign began, he said he did not expect Harlequins RL to break even in their first year and revealed the club had budgeted for a loss of £700,000, based on average gates of 4,000. However, he felt that if Quins could generate some kind of momentum and attract an average gate of 5,000, they would finish in the black, an amazing feat if they could pull it off. Lenagan was upbeat. However, he thought the real progress will be made in 2007. "I believe we could break even next year" he said. To take the club from administration to break even in two years will be a magnificent achievement."

And what would the club do with any profit, should they make any? "We have already agreed what the policy is for every extra £100,000 we make," said Lenagan. "I'm not looking to take profit out of the business. What the hell do I need profit out of a league club for? That is not why I am doing it. What we intend to do is put 50 per cent of any profit back into marketing, because we have a long-term aim to fill the stadium, and the other 50 per cent into buying new players."

Lenagan is clearly in it for the long haul but the home defeat to Wakefield must have been hard to stomach. In the corresponding fixture in 2005, which took place on 27 February, the Broncos had romped to a 72-8 victory. That loss sparked the beginning of the end for then Wildcats boss Shane McNally. He managed to last another four months before being given the boot, though not before giving one of the most memorable sporting quotes of 2005 in the wake of the 12-try thrashing by the Broncos. "Trying to explain this performance is like trying to row upstream in a barbed wire canoe," said the Australian. Twelve months on, it was countryman Rea who was left to find the right words to describe his side's dismal showing. "It was a very poor effort and we got what we deserved," he said. "Wakefield deserve a lot of credit, but we were very poor. We've got to get back on the training field and continue to work as hard as we can to improve and get the first win we desperately want."

Rea had met the Queen and Prince Phillip one afternoon leading up to the game. The get-together at Buckingham Palace, involving several high-profile Australians living and working in London, also attracted the likes of Clive James, Rolf Harris, Germaine Greer and Michael Lynagh. The invite had caught Rea by surprise, but he felt honoured to be in such esteemed company. "I had zero nerves, but I was full of intrigue," he recalled. "I didn't know whether it would be very formal – and it was – but the Queen and Prince Phillip were really warm people. We didn't have a great chat or anything, it was very much small talk, but I was pretty conscious of not knocking on when I said 'hello'." If only his players had been so fastidious when they came face to face with the likes of Tadulala and David Solomona just a few days later.

Rea refused to blame the pressure of performing on home turf for Harlequins RL's lacklustre showing against the Wildcats. He preferred to heap praise on the visitors. But Mark Tookey admitted the reverse had left a lot of the Quins players "looking for answers". Training, the prop said, had been good in the run-up to the game, although in retrospect he felt the players might have got too carried away. "Some of our sessions go to custard from over-excitement," he said. "Everyone needs to slow down and worry about the job ahead."

Tookey's words had an impact. The trip to Hull the following weekend promised to be another torrid affair. But the Quins, just as they had done at Odsal earlier in the season, showed amazing powers of recovery to register a shock 10-6 victory. "Unbelievable result," wrote one ecstatic Quins fan on one of the internet message boards. "We have beaten one of the fancied teams on their own patch. God knows how they did it but you have to hand it to them. How they turned it around after last week's abysmal performance escapes me."

The Friday night success at the Kingston Communications Stadium temporarily lifted Harlequins RL to sixth in the table and dispelled some of the dark clouds that had gathered over the Stoop in the wake of the defeat to Wakefield.

For Hull, the loss was a big setback. They had won two of their opening three games only to stumble against a side they would have expected to beat – and beat comfortably. It may not have been apparent at the time, but the defeat also marked the beginning of the end for coach John Kear. He might have led the club to their first trophy in 23 years just seven months previously, engineering a shock 25-24 defeat of favourites Leeds Rhinos in the final of the Challenge Cup, but he would last just five more weeks before becoming the first coaching casualty of the season.

The win at the KC Stadium was just the tonic Harlequins RL needed. Just as they had done at Bradford, they dug deep defensively after stunning the home team with two tries from Thomas Leuluai and Tyrone Smith inside five first-half minutes. Hull bounced back with a 50-metre score from Shaun Briscoe and continued to pressurise the visitors. But some hard hits and smart play from Quins in demanding conditions kept them at bay. "It took a lot of courage for the players to do what they did, they really pulled together as a group," enthused Rea. "They were tough and determined."

Keen to see how they responded after the Wakefield debacle, Rea had kept a close eye on his players in the run-up to the match at Hull. To help the healing process, he had kept things simple in training, steering clear of anything too challenging. It was a tactic the team was to adopt for the match itself. With the pitch having taken a real soaking from the rain, Rea and the players decided an hour before kick-off to change the way they would approach the game. Instead of chucking the ball about, they felt it was in their best interests to keep things nice and tight, and to avoid any moves that might result in handling errors. To Rea's delight, the players followed the new game plan to the letter. "They were real rock-solid," he said. "They didn't waver. Had one person wavered, it probably wouldn't have worked."

The effort took its toll on the team, just as it had done against Bradford. In the words of Tookey, the players were "stuffed". The

Sydney-born prop forward, in his second season in London, reckoned there was a 25-minute spell when Quins did not get out of their own half. "We would get to the fifth tackle and kick the hell out of the ball, but it only got to the halfway line and they would be back at us again," he said. "That happened continuously. They just kept coming." The loss of Sykes and Dorn to injury did not help Quins' cause, but they dug deep for their first victory.

Rea was happy with the win but far from satisfied with his side's early form. "We have some work to do," he said. "We have lacked a bit of focus in our play and I don't think we are getting where we want to be just yet. At the moment, we are just making sure we do the little things right that make the team function well. For example, I could get nothing out of the Wakefield game. We were so ordinary on the day there was so little I could take from it."

Nevertheless, he felt that confidence had been replenished by the win at Hull. The key now was to be consistent. "We have got everything that makes a good team but have got to put in the performances," he said. "It is still early days and, like most clubs, we are still finding our feet, but we haven't won back-to-back games as the Harlequins RL and have yet to win at The Stoop." The opportunity to rectify that last statistic would come the following Sunday when Tookey's old club Castleford made the trip to west London.

Mark McLinden – Harlequins RL team captain and a key player in 2006.
(Photo: David Williams)

3. Kitbags and comebacks

"I have spent a decent proportion of my life on National Express coaches. They are very underrated."
Steve Magee, Harlequins RL kitman

March had begun on an optimistic note for Harlequins RL with the victory at Hull. But from that moment on the month deteriorated rapidly for the London club. A run of three straight defeats, culminating in a 60-0 thrashing at home to Leeds Rhinos, was bad enough, leaving Quins just one place above bottom side Wigan Warriors in the Super League table. But a growing injury list threatened to throw the club into crisis.

One of the wounded was Paul Sykes. His injury, sustained in the win over Hull at the Kingston Communications Stadium, is the kind that places sport in perspective, quickly rendering a missed tackle or dropped pass unimportant. As the team headed back to the capital basking in the glow of their hard-earned 10-6 success, the 24-year-old centre was laid up in a hospital, not knowing whether he would play again and fearing the loss of a kidney. The cruel irony of it all was that he had only just returned to full fitness, having spent most of the off-season recuperating from knee surgery.

A vital cog in the Quins machine, Sykes had been talked of as a future Great Britain international at the end of 2005 following another successful season. The goalkicking centre had topped the scoring charts for the London Broncos with 288 points and was now the club's longest serving player, having originally joined on loan from Bradford Bulls in 2001 before making the move permanent in August 2002. His value to the team was clear, which is why his injury was all the more heartbreaking.

Sykes was not sure exactly how he ended up in intensive care. After tackling Sid Domic, he felt a sharp pain in his abdomen but thought he had jarred his ribs, or maybe broken one or two at worst. However, his discomfort increased, forcing him to seek refuge in the changing room. Sykes may not have been aware just how badly hurt he was, but Harlequins RL physiotherapist Tim Needham had a pretty good idea he was in a lot of trouble. "Paul played every minute of last season, except when he was sin-binned, so it must have been serious for him to come off," he said.

With club physician Dr Dee Jennings back in London, Sykes was initially looked after by Hull's doctor, Mark Higson. A kidney specialist, he recognised that Sykes may have damaged that particular area of his body and felt he needed to go to hospital to determine the true extent of the injury. By now, Sykes was getting a little worried. When the subsequent diagnosis revealed that one of his kidneys had been punctured, concern turned to shock. "I really thought I had broken one of my ribs," he said. "I wasn't expecting this at all."

Rea spoke for everyone at Harlequins RL when it emerged just how ill Sykes was. "Paul's long-term health is our main concern," he said. "We're not even thinking at this stage about football. I've been checking regularly that he is responding to treatment and that his spirits are okay."

Mentally, Sykes was not in bad shape, although, unable to train, his weight quickly plummeted from 15 stones to 12-and-a-half. He knew he was unlikely to play again in 2006, but his chief concern was his health – and escaping the boredom that inevitably came with being laid up in a hospital bed for more than a couple of days. After a week in Hull, he was able to transfer to Wakefield to be closer to his family and friends in Dewsbury. Eventually, after he had stopped passing blood when he urinated, he was discharged. His mobility remained limited, while coughing and laughing were definite no-nos. But now it was simply a question of waiting. His doctors said he was making good progress but he was not yet out of the woods. He would have to wait two months before getting the all-clear.

Back in London, Harlequins RL began preparing for the visit of Castleford on 12 March. Tony Rea's side were still chasing their first win at the Twickenham Stoop. Understandably, many Quins fans thought the game with the Tigers was the perfect opportunity to break the barren run at home. Their opponents, back in the top flight after a brief absence, had lost three of their opening four games and were tipped to make an instant return to the National League. But there was the nagging feeling that Quins were still vulnerable, that they could be brilliant one week and woeful the next. The attitude and defensive effort at Hull had pleased Rea immensely, the shattered bodies in the dressing room convincing him that they had given everything asked of them. But no one was exactly sure what to expect. There was already talk of a home jinx. The clash with Castleford had added spice, too. In charge of the Tigers was Terry Matterson, a former London Broncos captain and a good friend of Rea. Matterson had taken over in the off-season, replacing fellow Australian Dave Woods, who had been unmercifully sacked despite guiding the club to promotion.

Rea must have felt his fears were unfounded when Quins raced into a 14-0 lead over Castleford after just 13 minutes. Lee Hopkins, skippering the side in the continued absence of Mark McLinden, had

Castleford comeback stuns Quins

Top: Lee Hopkins scoring – Quins were 14-0 up in 14 minutes.
Middle: Hopkins celebrates with Tyrone Smith.
Bottom: Quins fans celebrate – they thought their team was heading for a win. (All photos: Peter Lush)

Daniel Heckenberg completes a tackle.

Heading for the line. In the background the frame of the new South Stand at Twickenham is visible.

Danny Williams being tackled while going for the line. Quins were ahead 20-16 at half-time, but lost 20-34. (All photos: Peter Lush)

touched down twice, while Tony Clubb, getting stronger with every game he played, raced 80 yards for an interception try as Quins threatened to run away with the match. Alas, the Tigers did not fold but bashed and crashed their way back into the contest, with the two Dannys, Sculthorpe and Ward, very much to the fore. By half-time - and despite a brilliant try from Thomas Leuluai - Cas had reduced the deficit to just four points. The momentum was to remain firmly with the visitors. Quins lost their shape, their kicking game seemed to disintegrate, they knocked on repeatedly and they failed to complete sets. Cas, on other hand, seemed to grow in confidence and stature as they made ever-easier yards. Such was their dominance that Quins failed to score a single point in the second half. The home side's woe was compounded by the loss of Rob Purdham to a shoulder injury and Luke Dorn to the sin-bin, the latter penalised for a professional foul on Gray Viane. When the Tigers scored their final try of the match, Andy Henderson crossing after 73 minutes, their bench leapt as one, knowing victory was theirs. In sharp contrast, Rea stood motionless in front of the home dugout, his hands in his pockets and a grim look on his face.

The Castleford supporters had been vocal throughout the afternoon. They had congregated in the North Stand for the first half and walked en masse to the far end of the Lexus Stand after the break in order to be get a closer view of what they hoped would be more tries for their side. They were not to be disappointed, either with the performance of their own side or the facilities around them. One fan, bearing an uncanny resemblance to comedian Peter Kay, was almost rendered speechless by the toilets in the Lexus Stand. Not only were they mould-free, there was somewhere to put your pint - pure bliss.

Rea preferred to pay tribute to Castleford rather than publicly lambaste his own team when he faced the media after the 30-24 defeat. "Full credit to them, they threw more at us than we threw at them," he said. "They played some great footie with a lot of spirit. We weren't a team today, apart from the first 20 minutes."

Unsurprisingly, the post-match presentation in the Kings Bar had a hollow feel to it. Following the two previous home games, the entire Quins team had awaited disconsolately to find out which of them had won the man-of-the-match awards on offer, voted for by the sponsors and players respectively. But on this occasion, only Hopkins appeared. Much as announcer Chris Warren tried to keep the mood upbeat, he acknowledged that his stock question - "Where did it all go wrong?" - was becoming a little tiresome.

Hopkins was in no mood to pull any punches, perhaps sensing it would be futile to try to convince the fans that this had been anything but a woeful display. In a frank admission, the Australian apologised for the "embarrassing" performance before trudging off to rejoin his team-mates, who were already tucking into their post-match meal.

While the players cleaned their plates, Quins kitman Steve Magee was left to clean the home changing room. Strewn on the floor, in amongst the benches and hot and cold plunge pools, were half-eaten orange segments, discarded water bottles, used strapping torn off various parts of the body and 17 kits, muddied and stretched. His day had started much earlier than the players – and it would finish much later, too.

Magee is one of the club's unsung heroes. He has been involved from the very start, as head groundsman at Craven Cottage back in 1980. Football was his main love then, in particular Fulham FC. He went on to attend 1,076 consecutive first-team matches between 1976 and 1996 as well as several reserve games. But he also took an instant liking to rugby league. He liked its bluntness and the way the players mixed with supporters after games. Now he is very much part of the furniture, though never hard to miss. His long flowing hair is pulled back into a ponytail while he is often seen sporting a luminous green tee-shirt, usually when he runs onto the pitch with the kicking tee. Plenty of people have told him his flowing mane is past its sell-by date - chief among them former coach Ross Strudwick - but Magee remains oblivious, happy with his own sense of style.

Speak to Magee for any length of time and his respect for structure and order soon becomes apparent. He does not refer to Rea by name but as "coach", just as he did with Rea's predecessors. In many ways, Magee belongs to a bygone era. Yet he remains at the very core of the club as it seeks to make its mark in the 21st century. He is more than just a kitman, he is the heartbeat of the club. The club may have lurched from one crisis to another, but he has been a constant and reliable figure.

Sport needs people like Magee. They keep it honest, ensure it never loses touch with reality. There are numerous Magees scattered about, those who devote large chunks of their lives to their local clubs. But London's version is special.

In terms of dedication to the cause, Magee takes some beating. As head groundsman at Fulham he often found himself working into the night on a Saturday transforming the pitch. Floodlights on, he would remove the football markings and paint the white lines required for the rugby league match the next day before changing the posts and advertising boards.

After leaving Craven Cottage the club found itself at the Polytechnic Stadium in Chiswick. Magee led an army of volunteers charged with ensuring the ground was up to scratch. Ask him what he remembers from that period and he will talk about a special era when people gave up their spare time to keep the club going. None more so than Magee, who once found himself cycling from Fulham to Chiswick with a can of paint on either side of his handlebars and a paintbrush perched in the middle.

But his loyalty was really put to the test when the club found itself at the National Sports Centre at Crystal Palace for the second time in 1990. That's when he became kitman for the first time, agreeing to Strudwick's request to assume added team responsibilities while remaining the football club's head groundsman at Craven Cottage. Magee, who liked and respected the Australian, was happy to oblige, not realising just what he had let himself in for.

Life was not too bad for Magee when both the football and rugby league teams were playing at home. His tasks were just about manageable. But when the football team was at home one day and the rugby league team was away the next, he quickly found himself being stretched to breaking point as he tried to fulfil his commitments to both.

Magee's problems started when the rugby league team decided to travel to an away game in the north on a Saturday, choosing to stay overnight in a hotel before the match on the Sunday. His duties at Craven Cottage meant he could not join them on the team bus. Instead, already tired and a little dishevelled, he would have to make his own way north.

His work done in Fulham, Magee would head off across London to Victoria Station, where he would board a National Express coach leaving the capital at 10pm. He would eventually arrive somewhere like Carlisle at 4.25am, when he would head for the nearest park bench or station platform to get some much-needed shut-eye. Then, somewhat refreshed, he would link up with the team, who had spent the night tucked up in a hotel bed and were looking forward to a breakfast of eggs, bacon, sausages, toast and tea. "Sometimes I would take a walk around the town as I waited for the first train or bus on Sunday morning that would take me towards to the team hotel," recalled Magee. If the team were playing at Guildford Park in Carlisle, he would walk to the stadium and sneak a few hours of sleep in the changing rooms before the team arrived.

It would not surprise anyone if Magee refused to take another coach journey in his life. People have developed phobias for less. However, he has nothing but praise for that mode of travel. "I have spent a decent proportion of my life on National Express coaches," he said. "They are very underrated." What's more, Magee financed all the trips north himself and only started receiving recompense for his regular night-time odysseys in 1993. All so that he could fulfil his promise to Strudwick to look after the team's kit.

Magee is a methodical character and well suited to his job. A Super League team is in a constant state of flux, endlessly preparing for, travelling to and playing games. To ensure he never misses a trick, he carries a notebook with him at all times in which he details everything he needs to do. Besides washing the kit, which he does at a coin-op laundry a 20-minute walk from the Twickenham Stoop, he attends to a lot of the players' needs, picking up prescriptions and ensuring they have plenty of fruit to eat at training. He arrives early and leaves late, helping lay the equipment out before a session and then packing it away afterwards. A fair percentage of his time is spent ferrying it between the Stoop and the training ground at Roehampton Vale.

It took Magee, with the help of timekeeper Barry Fenn, several hours to restore order to the Quins changing room after the defeat to Castleford. Eventually he transported everything into his trailer at The Stoop. Magee regularly works more than 100 hours a week, more like 120 when the team are playing away. By the time he slumped into his chair in the lock-up, he was exhausted and could no longer keep his eyes open. His bed may have been just a few miles away in Kingston, but he could not budge. He set the alarm on his mobile for 4.30am and fell asleep.

Neil Budworth had watched the Castleford game from the sidelines, a role to which he had become increasingly accustomed since sustaining a serious knee injury in March 2005 against Wigan, his former club, at Griffin Park. On that day, Paul Sykes was in top form, scoring 22 points as the Broncos ran out 34-20 winners. But midway through the first half, Budworth had limped out of the fray after tackling Martin Aspinwall. He had tried to push the Wigan player to the side to slow down the play-the-ball, but his knee buckled to the left. "I knew something was wrong when I got up and ran back to the line," he recalled. "I thought maybe I could run through it but my knee collapsed when I was less than a metre from the player running at me. That was it, the defining moment."

A scan showed that Budworth had ruptured the anterior cruciate ligament. He would need surgery and was told he would be sidelined for six months. After the operation, he returned to his native Wigan, where he spent a lot of time in bed for the next two weeks, his knee packed with ice and his family doing a lot of running around for him.

Six months later, with his recovery going to plan, he made another trip home. It was then that his problems started. His knee began giving him pain after each training session and failed to improve after he was given a cortisone injection. Budworth was eventually told he would require another operation, and on 21 December went under the knife again. "I did not have a great Christmas," he admitted. However, his determination never wavered. His knee improved and he began to dream of playing again. It became clear he would miss the start of the 2006 season, but he was closing in fast on a return. Finally, he was given the green light to join in training again. "I could not stop smiling, I was loving it," he said. There was light at the end of the tunnel for the hooker. The day before the Castleford match, he had made his long-awaited return to action in an under-21s game.

Harlequins RL had started the season without two of their three hookers. Budworth was out and so was new signing Chad Randall. The son of Manly Sea Eagles legend Terry was forced to miss the first few weeks after undergoing a shoulder reconstruction. So the hooking duties fell solely upon Pat Weisner, another close-season capture. An Australian, Weisner had a successful 2005 campaign with Halifax and had made the National League 1 Dream Team. Still, it was asking a lot for a player with no Super League experience to fill such a crucial position on his own. Rea had been impressed with Weisner's contribution in the opening weeks of the season, but the return of Budworth and Randall was set to boost his options.

Budworth says the key facets of a good hooker are strong defence, good passing and speed around the ruck area. He describes these as the "principles of my play" and says that if a hooker can learn when to run and when to pass, it can prove crucial in helping a team's go-forward. He finally got the chance to put his skills to the test against Castleford's under-21s on Saturday 11 March. He could barely contain his excitement at the prospect of finally playing again. "I was a bit nervous before but as soon as the game started I felt fairly comfortable," he said. He was involved from the start, making the second tackle of the game and looking to involve himself as often as possible. He played for 70 minutes in total and was happy with his performance. It was a satisfying moment after all the effort he had put in to his rehabilitation. "My goal was to get back as quickly as I could," he said. "I think I have stuck to that goal well."

Back in the swing of things, Budworth hoped a return to Super League action would not be too far away. It wasn't. To his delight, he was included in the 17-man squad to face Huddersfield at the Galpharm Stadium on 19 March. So was Chad Randall. Things were looking up.

Matt Gafa – a new recruit from Australia – in action against Bradford. (Photo: David Williams)

If the game against the Giants represented a personal triumph for Budworth, it marked a real low for Quins. Jon Sharp's team were one point better off than their London rivals, having beaten Warrington and Wakefield in their first five Super League games. They had also pushed St Helens all the way the weekend before, eventually losing by two points.

Quins started brightly. Wearing their white away shirt for the first time, they fell behind to a Chris Thorman penalty but scored the first try through former Salford half-back Tim Hartley when he collected a wonderfully weighted grubber kick from Thomas Leuluai. Stephen Wild replied for the Giants before Zebastian Luisi, so impressive through the opening weeks of the campaign, scored his first try of the season to help Quins into a 12-8 lead. From that point on, however, the game plan disintegrated as the home team, led by Thorman and Robbie Paul, took total control. By the time Budworth replaced Randall after 25 minutes, Huddersfield had levelled the scores through a James Evans try. By the break, the visitors had started to fall off tackles and were trailing 22-14.

The second half was a disaster. Quins failed to score while Sharp's team ran in a further seven tries to emerge victorious by 50 points. Jon Wells was summarising for BBC Radio London as he continued his rehabilitation from a foot injury sustained in pre-season. The 28-year-old winger, not afraid of ruffling a few feathers, was scathing in his criticism of his team-mates. Midway through the second half, he barked: "There is no professionalism, they are just trying to hurt the opposition. We are not playing rugby any more and need to take a long, hard look at ourselves."

As if the 64-14 defeat was not punishment enough, Luisi had been stretchered from the field in the second half with a damaged left shoulder, the full-back joining Karl Temata and Lee Hopkins on the sidelines. It was the injuries and the way his team had crumbled as a result that upset Tony Rea. "The worst thing - and I don't like it - was that the injuries affected our performance," he said. "A lot of people said that was why we lost but I was frustrated we let a couple of injuries get the better of us."

After scrutinising the video of the Huddersfield game with assistant Rohan Smith, Rea saw his players down at Roehampton Vale the following week and went through it again. It was a painful process. The players expect to be shown a replay of a match whatever the result, but it becomes an emotionally draining experience after a defeat. It can be hard for players to have their mistakes highlighted in front of their team-mates.

Rob Purdham had missed the game against Huddersfield because of injury, but he was at the video session. He felt that the standard of defence had been unacceptable. Quins had been steamrollered after the break and had made far too many individual errors. He also felt that the team needed to start concentrating for the full 80 minutes.

Quins were now languishing near the foot of the table after losing four of their first six league games. It did not look as though their situation would improve the coming weekend either, when Leeds Rhinos were to visit the Twickenham Stoop.

By the time the Rhinos arrived in west London on Saturday 25 March, the mood in the Quins camp had lightened. Training had gone well while the players had started growing beards in honour of Mark Tookey, which had raised a few laughs. However, the injury list was a real problem. Mark McLinden, Wells, Sykes and Purdham were joined on the sidelines by Rikki Sheriffe, Solomon Haumono, Luisi and Temata.

Rea called for "strength and solidarity" and tried to stress the positives, one of which was that the loss of certain players would give some of the youngsters a chance to prove themselves. Louie McCarthy-Scarsbrook, a 20-year-old prop from Lewisham, Michael Worrincy, a 20-year-old loose-forward who had learned his trade at Greenwich Admirals, and Duncan James, a 21-year-old rugby union scrum-half, were all named in his 20-man squad, though only McCarthy-Scarsbrook actually played against the Rhinos. In contrast, Leeds would go into the game boosted by the return of Great Britain skipper Jamie Peacock. Only Jamie Jones-Buchanan and former West Tigers captain Mark O'Neill were missing from their first-team squad.

The match turned out to be a spectacle of clinical rugby by a brilliant team in scintillating form. Danny McGuire underlined his return to form with four first-half tries as the visitors, undeterred by the wet conditions, ran riot after a tight first 10 minutes. Six of their 10 tries came in the opening 40 minutes, leaving Quins in a state of shock. One rugby union fan, attending his first league match, was bowled over by the skill on display. Had an international union side played with such verve and veracity, he remarked, everyone would have been "cooing with delight".

At first glance, the result was another disaster for Harlequins RL. The defeat, screened live by Sky, meant Quins had conceded 124 points in their last two games and had just three points to show from their opening seven games of the competition. All the pre-season talk of repeating their top-six finish in 2005 started to have a hollow ring to it. What's more, the enthusiasm generated by the move to the Stoop had quickly worn off. Worryingly, chief executive Nic Cartwright felt the wave of interest created at the start of the season had "almost died". He insisted a lot of targets had been met but recognised that the club would really only flourish if it started winning games.

Rea insisted it was not all doom and gloom. He felt the team had improved after the dismal showing at Huddersfield and insisted there was plenty to build on. It had been a difficult month, after the bright opening against Hull, but he remained upbeat.

Leeds captain Kevin Sinfield was not so sure Rea's players felt the same way. When he shook hands with Lee Hopkins after the final hooter, he could see the pain of defeat etched on the Australian's face. According to Sinfield, Hopkins looked "completely devastated". Nevertheless, he thought Quins would recover and, ever the optimist, pointed out that they were still only three points off a play-off spot. Still, Quins had now lost their opening four home games of the season. If they were going to make inroads, they needed to turn the Twickenham Stoop into a fortress. At the moment it resembled a sandcastle.

The Quins players were pretty downbeat as they headed for home. But there was some cheer for Budworth when he turned on his mobile phone and discovered he had received a load of text messages. His mates had watched the game on television and were far from impressed with the goatee he was sporting. "Little Mark Tookey" was the thrust of the abuse, but it made him smile.

Thomas Leuluai escapes the clutches of Bradford's Stuart Fielden.

Brian McDermott has high hopes for David Mills (left) in 2007, while Chad Randall (right) will be looking to build on his solid finish to 2006. (All photos: David Williams)

4. Hypodermics to hyperthermia

"The players are like my extended family. I treat them all as my sons."
Dr Dee Jennings, Harlequins RL club doctor

Rainwater trickled down a drainpipe at Teddington station in south west London. It was a typical spring afternoon, with intermittent showers punctuated by bursts of pleasant, soothing sunshine. The weather, however, was not the topic under discussion as a group of Harlequins RL supporters waited with growing frustration on Park Road. The essential engineering works being carried out by South West Trains on that first Sunday in April was making the journey to the Twickenham Stoop an arduous and stressful one.

Quins were due to play Challenge Cup fourth-round opponents Toulouse in less than an hour, but the promised rail replacement bus service was nowhere in sight. Platform staff at Vauxhall station earlier in the afternoon had been a little sketchy when it came to providing information about alternative means of getting to the Stoop. Rumours of a bus service from Teddington to Twickenham had persuaded some Quins fans to head there. Now, as they wondered just when they would get to the ground, they began reminiscing about past transport woes.

Two fans talked in almost nostalgic terms about an emergency taxi dash across London for a game against Wigan. Or was it Bradford? They were having troubling remembering the details. Eventually, 40 minutes before the match against Toulouse was due to kick off, a bus appeared and began to wind its way towards the Stoop for the first cup tie of the new era.

Toulouse had created shockwaves in 2005 by becoming the first French side to reach the semi-finals of the Challenge Cup. They had upset then Super League side Widnes Vikings in the last eight before going down to Leeds Rhinos, who eventually lost in the final to Hull FC.

However, the Toulouse team that made the trek to west London on 2 April 2006 was not the force of a year ago. They had lost many of their best players while their coach, Justin Morgan, had crossed The Channel soon after their amazing cup run had come to an end in order to take charge of National League 1 side Hull Kingston Rovers. Quins insisted they would treat their opponents with respect, but few expected Toulouse to pose any kind of threat.

The Challenge Cup represented Harlequins RL's best chance of success in 2006. They had hopes of reaching the Super League play-offs, but a possible trip to Wembley was a very realistic goal, as long as the draw was kind to them.

The club had reached the final in 1999, only to lose 52-16 to Leeds Rhinos. Yet the day remains one of the most memorable in its history. The now defunct supporters' club had celebrated the occasion by hiring an open-top bus to take some fans on a nostalgic trip past some of the venues that had at one time or another been called home. Starting out at Victoria station, the double decker, covered in banners, flags and balloons, had made its way to Craven Cottage, past the Polytechnic Stadium in Chiswick and on to the Stoop, the club's home ground at the time. The final leg of the journey took the bus to Wembley.

For the vast majority of the Broncos fans, the feat of making the final in 1999 was almost inconceivable. "Being there was something beyond our wildest dreams," wrote Peter Lush in the book *From Fulham to Wembley*, an account of the club's first 20 years. "Coming out of the station at Wembley, seeing all the support for the club, I took some photos to make sure that I was not dreaming."

The players were overawed, too. For Broncos legend Steele Retchless it was the greatest moment of his career. "We didn't have much success but we had some great times and that final was a truly great memory," enthused the Australian, who had played no small part in helping the team reach Wembley. In a thrilling semi-final at Headingley, he had scored the try that had sunk Castleford, slicing through the Tigers defence in the 80th minute to clinch a dramatic 33-27 victory.

Perhaps the most surprising reaction, though, came from Shaun Edwards. He had already played in a record-breaking 10 Challenge Cup Finals with Wigan, winning nine of them, yet to get there with the Broncos had given him an extra-special feeling. "When I used to get to the final with Wigan, it was relief more than anything else. We were expected to get there," said the legendary scrum-half, who was in his second spell with the Broncos at the time. "But for a club like London to make it gave complete and total elation."

Edwards maintains to this day that the Broncos could have won the final, pointing out that they only trailed 20-16 with 20 minutes to go. He says a broken thumb hampered his own play, affecting his passing and distribution, while the loss of props Grant Young and Darren Bradstreet in the run-up to the game meant some members of the team were forced to play out of position. Despite those setbacks, Edwards felt the Broncos had been in with a shout of victory. Reading between the lines, he was less than happy with the role of coach Dan Stains. The former Australian international prop had not coached at the top level before and had been dogged by rumours that he had trouble maintaining morale and handling the high-profile players. Edwards refuses to single out Stains directly for criticism, but you get the distinct impression he feels the outcome might have been different had assistant coach Les Kiss been given a little bit more influence. Retchless is not so sure, though. "We were massive underdogs," he said. "We had no fit front rowers. Shane Millard and I found ourselves in the front row at one stage. We didn't have much of a chance."

Edwards plies his trade in rugby union nowadays - he is head coach of leading English side Wasps - but he still has a lot of fondness for London's top league club. He took his son to the opening game of the 2006 season and admitted he felt a pang of jealousy as he walked around the Stoop. "It is a fantastic stadium now," he said. "It wasn't like this when I first joined." He also had nothing but praise for the partnership with the NEC Harlequins, insisting: "It is the biggest chance the club have ever had."

Ian Lenagan revealed on the eve of the 2006 season that one of his major goals was to lead Harlequins RL on to the pitch at Wembley prior to a Challenge Cup Final. He had seen Richard Branson and David Hughes do it in 1999 and hoped one day it would be him. "We don't know if we will do it this year but if there is one thing we want to win with a passion it is the Challenge Cup," Lenagan said before the season started. "Wembley is in our home city and we were there the last time the final was played there. I would dearly love to lead the team out."

By the time the fourth-round tie against Toulouse was played - Super League clubs only enter the competition at this stage - talk of Wembley had become redundant. The stadium was still being rebuilt and the date for its completion had been pushed back and back because of a series of setbacks. Finally, Australian contractors Multiplex had been forced to admit that Wembley would not be open for business again until 2007. The Rugby Football League reacted swiftly to the news. Recognising that thousands of rugby league fans had already booked accommodation in the capital, they switched the final to Twickenham. The disappointment was tangible. Wembley had been a massive draw. Yet for Harlequins, the lure of Twickenham still had huge appeal. The home of the Rugby Football Union, which had hosted the final in 2000, is just a stone's throw from the Stoop.

Harlequins RL expected a modest turn-out for the game against Toulouse, so only the East Stand was open to the spectators who turned up, all 1,245 of them. It was all a far cry from the previous day's drama at the Stoop when NEC Harlequins had won promotion back to English rugby union's top flight by beating Sedgley Park 65-8. Wild scenes of celebration had followed the victory and several stewards at the ground on Sunday looked distinctly the worse for wear. One of them, gazing bleary-eyed at the heavy pitch, concluded that despite all the rain overnight there was still more champagne on it than water.

A win over Toulouse was never going to produce a repeat of the previous night's festivities, but victory was just as vital. Not only would it put Quins a step closer to their dream of an appearance in the final, it would finally end their wait for a win at the Stoop and go some way to banishing memories of the 60-0 thrashing by Leeds in their previous match at home.

With talk of a home jinx having gathered momentum with every reverse at The Stoop, the Quins players were understandably a little nervous going into the game. When Nick Bradley-Qalilawa knocked on in their first set of six, allowing the visitors to open the scoring with a try from David Myles, the tension increased a notch or two.

Quins hit back with tries from Tony Clubb and Tyrone Smith, but they only led by four points at the interval. However, their superior fitness and ability told in the second half. They ran in seven unanswered tries, two of them from 18-year-old winger Clubb to give him his first senior hat-trick in only his fifth game.

The small group of journalists waiting for the post-match press conference to start in the media room could hear the Quins players singing their victory song in their dressing room. When Tony Rea finally emerged, he was just as ebullient. "We pretty much owned the field in terms of possession," he said. "The last couple of games were pretty disappointing, but no one sulked. I'm really happy and there is a buzz in the changing room."

The game also represented a personal triumph for Quins skipper Mark McLinden. He had missed his side's first seven games of the season after limping out of the warm-up prior to the opening match against St Helens. The initial diagnosis was a pulled hamstring, but, after making an unsuccessful attempt to return against Castleford a month later, it was clear there was more to the injury than first thought. As McLinden had prepared to take to the field for the warm-up prior to the game against the Tigers, club doctor Dee Jennings had warned him he was rushing back too soon. "But it was not something I wanted to hear and I asked her to be a little supportive," said McLinden. Minutes later, with his pride dented, he headed disconsolately back to the changing room. It would be another three weeks before he would play again.

It turned out that McLinden's injury was more complicated that a simple hamstring strain. The root of the problem was a bulging disc that was pressing on the sciatic nerve, giving the impression that he may have damaged his hamstring. This time, McLinden listened to what Dr Jennings had to tell him – and the advice he got was to rest. Dr Jennings had some degree of sympathy for McLinden, but not much. "Certain injuries are annoying because they drag on," she said. "Unfortunately, athletes are very impatient and tend to come back too soon. Then they wonder why they break down again."

Dr Jennings - or Dr Dee as the players know her - has been involved with London's top rugby league club since 1990. A general practitioner, she was spending some of her Wednesday afternoons at the Sports Injury Clinic at Crystal Palace when she bumped into Ross Strudwick, the former Brisbane Broncos coach who had taken over as coach of Fulham, as Quins were then known, in July 1989. The Australian needed a doctor to look after his team who were now playing at the National Sports Centre and asked is she would come to his aid. Dr Dee said she would ask around to see if anyone was interested, but Strudwick was not going to take 'no' for an answer. "I was conned by Ross," claimed Dr Dee. "He gave me some sob story about not having a doctor and told me if he couldn't find one his team wouldn't be able to play. So with considerable anxiety and foreboding, I agreed." Dr Dee thought it would be a temporary posting. Sixteen years on, she is still tending to the players' battered and bruised bodies.

Dr Dee has turned out to be much more than just a physician to the club. A spare room at her home is still called the Struddy Suite, a consequence of the amount of time that Strudwick, his wife and four children spent with the Jennings family while he was coach of the club. Numerous players have stayed there over the years, too, mainly the Antipodeans. "The players are like my extended family," she says. "I treat them all as my sons. When rugby league was a winter sport, a lot of them had nowhere to go for Christmas, so they would come round for dinner."

She remains in contact with a lot of the club's former players, such as Australian Scott Roskell. The former winger regularly emails her from his new home in New York, while his photograph is still displayed in her house. However, there are times when she tries to keep players at arm's length. "They call me about all sorts of things," she said. "Sometimes it's because their wife has had a baby and they want some advice or because one of their family has a bad cold. I try not to look after their families if I can and encourage them to register with a practice. But sometimes I think they just want to compare notes after they have seen someone else."

On match-days, Dr Dee arrives at the Stoop 90 minutes before kick-off. Her first job is to ensure the paramedics are in place and briefed. Then she turns her attention to the players. She works closely with the physiotherapists, often administering last-minute treatment before the team heads out onto the pitch for the warm-up and then the match. "Often it is a question of deciding whether a player can play or whether he needs a painkiller," she says.

If a player is injured during the game, Dr Dee only gets involved if it looks like it could be serious and the physiotherapist has asked for help. "It has to be bad for me to go on," she says. If the player eventually picks himself up and carries on playing, there is not much more for her to do. But if he has been forced to leave the field, either under his own steam or on a stretcher, she has to decide the next course of action. Does the player need to go to hospital immediately for treatment? Does the injury need X-raying? Often it is a case of making the player comfortable and then referring him to a specialist.

Dr Dee cares a lot about the players, but rugby league is not her only passion. A union fan who still holds a debenture seat at the Stoop for the XV-a-side game, she is also the chief doctor for the British Judo Association and has travelled with the team to the Olympic Games in Atlanta (1996), Sydney (2000) and Athens (2004). Her work in sport has won her recognition from the Royal Society of Medicine but awards do not mean much to her. "I don't hang on to things like that," she says.

Under her supervision, McLinden came through the Challenge Cup tie with Toulouse unscathed, but he would face a far sterner threat to his physical well-being the following weekend, when Harlequins RL travelled to Super League leaders St Helens, who were still unbeaten in 2006.

It was not so much that McLinden could expect to spend much of the game making tackle after tackle in an effort to keep Saints at bay, though that is what happened. Instead, it was the driving wind and heavy rain that conspired to push the Australian to the very limits of his capabilities. By the second half of the game at Knowsley Road on Friday 7 April he was so cold he had to ask Quins' assistant coach Mark Barnes if he could lay his hands on a set of 'skins' – the special clothing that the players often wear in training to keep them warm. It turned out there was only one set available – and they were being worn by the assistant coach. Barnes had no hesitation in stripping off, but by the time McLinden put the gear on, he was beyond saving. "I was so cold already that they didn't really do me much good," said the full-back.

McLinden lasted until the 75th minute. When he was finally substituted, he headed straight for the changing room. His team was still in with a chance of victory, but the Australian knew that, for once, his priorities lay elsewhere. He walked straight into the showers, not bothering to take his kit off, and stood under the hot spray, willing the feeling to return to his body. The rest of the squad arrived shortly after the final hooter sounded and, like their captain, most did not bother to dispense with their shirts and shorts before stepping into the showers. Normally, the players would take turns dipping in and out of the hot and cold plunge pools following a game, but this was not a normal day. "One or two forwards had an ice bath but most of us had had one of those all game," said McLinden. "There wasn't much said about the game because our priority was to get warm."

Harlequins RL were beaten 16-6 by Saints but it was, in the eyes of the Quins coaching staff, their best performance of the season. They had led 6-4 early on thanks to McLinden's 100th career try and Matt Gafa's conversion. Saints only sealed victory with eight minutes to go, James Graham's try putting the game beyond the reach of the visitors. "Anytime you can keep Saints to 16 points, whether it is wet, dry or snowing, has to be pretty rewarding for a defensive unit," said Quins assistant coach Rohan Smith. "The conditions were bad and inhibited how St Helens played, but it was only 10-6 with not long to go."

Despite praise from Smith, McLinden was not happy. He felt his side had thrown away the chance of a much-needed win. The defeat at Saints left Harlequins RL with just one win from their first eight league games and deep in trouble at the wrong end of the table. "We blew a couple of tries," said the skipper. "Lee Hopkins dropped the ball over the line in the wet and then Gafa almost grounded the ball. We were definitely in there and competing."

McLinden, with his blond hair and chiselled good looks, is fast becoming a big favourite with Quins fans. Skilful and gutsy on the pitch, charming and professional off it, he is the epitome of what rugby league supporters like in a player.

Born in Canberra on 8 July 1979, he grew up playing touch rugby with his family, who joined forces with their neighbours, the Smiths, to form the 'McSmiths' touch team.

McLinden played union at first but switched codes after watching the 1989 Grand Final between Canberra Raiders, his hometown team, and Balmain Tigers, the red-hot favourites. For some reason, McLinden chose to support the Tigers while the rest of his family backed the Raiders. By half-time - Balmain, who had a certain Shaun Edwards in their side, were leading 12-2. But Canberra went on to stage one of the great comebacks, winning 19-14 in extra-time in what is widely regarded as one of the best finals ever. From that moment on, McLinden had his heart set on becoming a Raider.

McLinden made an immediate impact in league and soon came to the attention of Canberra, who sent a talent scout to his house to discuss his future. "I was very nervous because they were effectively offering me a contract, so I appointed dad as my manager," recalled McLinden, who was 16 at the time. "I was still going to school but they offered me $50 a week. I thought I was worth more. I told them that my mum drove me to training every day, which to me was worth an extra $20 a week. They agreed and I thought I had done well, but, looking back, the guy from the Raiders must have been thinking 'Gee that was cheap'."

McLinden was encouraged to continue his studies by his parents while he pursued his career with Canberra, but it quickly became clear he was a star on the rugby league pitch. A junior with West Belconnen Warriors, he won the SG Ball under-17 Premiership with the Raiders in 1995 and was chosen to play for the Australian Schoolboys in 1996.

It was around that time that he received a telephone call that changed his life. Initially he thought his PE teacher was winding him up when he was told that the Canberra head coach was on the line and wanted to talk to him. It wasn't just any old head coach either. Mal Meninga remains one of the game's greatest players, his bulldozing runs and match-winning plays giving him superstar status in both hemispheres. He captained Australia 23 times and played 45 games for his country. He also led Canberra to three Grand Final victories in three years, including the 1989 triumph that had such an impact on a young McLinden. In fact, it was Meninga's nerveless conversion against Balmain that sent the game into added time.

Meninga wanted McLinden to train with the senior team. It was a golden opportunity – and one the youngster was not about to let slip through his fingers. A professional deal soon followed. Then in 1998 came his debut season in first grade. It went better than he could have expected and he was named the National Rugby League's Rookie of the Year. "It was just a dream," said McLinden. "People were so supportive because I was a home-grown product. It was very special for me. There were people who had tracked my progress for years. I knew something extraordinary had happened but I did not really know what it was."

McLinden lived at home during his debut season and was mixing with players whose photos adorned his bedroom walls. It was a bit daunting at first, turning up for training with the likes of Bradley Clyde, Ricky Stuart and Laurie Daley, and he admits it was not easy to settle in. After his first session with the senior squad, he was pulled to one side by Daley. "I'd called him by his surname during one of the ball drills and he told me 'it's not Daley, it's Lozzer'," recalled McLinden. "I was a bit out of my depth at the start."

McLinden, who began his Raiders career as a full-back before moving to the halves, was a regular in the side for the next seven years. Unfortunately for him, the club had lost its aura of invincibility. A number of its star players had departed, among them former Australia captain Daley, who was forced to retire from the game in 2000 because of injury. McLinden admits it was hard to live up to the high expectations of the Canberra fans, but he praised them for their patience. "You were trying your best to fill Daley's shoes but the community knew it was going to take time to get a team like they had in 1994," he said.

McLinden loved nothing more than representing his home-town team but by 2004 he was considering a fresh challenge. Many of his mates had travelled overseas after finishing their studies and he wanted to see some of the world too. Castleford came in with an offer but McLinden was not convinced it was the best move for him. He was also a little reticent at leaving his ageing grandmother behind. After much thought, he decided to stay put and signed a new three-year deal with the Raiders.

A year later – and his wanderlust reignited by an end-of-season break in the United States – his desire to leave Canberra became unquenchable. McLinden called his manager, who immediately started making enquiries on his behalf. Several Super League clubs showed an interest, but he agreed to sign for the Broncos. One of the first people he told was his mother. She was over the moon. Unfortunately, she thought he had meant Brisbane not London. Instead of seeing more of her son now she had moved from Canberra to the Queensland capital, she would have to make do with the odd telephone call or e-mail.

The performance at St Helens on 7 April had given Harlequins RL great encouragement for the rest of the season. McLinden was both pleased and relieved. In the first few weeks of the campaign, he felt the players were not as focused as they should have been. Now, though, he felt the intensity was back. The players were looking sharp and listening more attentively to what Tony Rea had to say. "The coach can talk to us until his heart's content, but none of it will have an affect unless players make a decision to take it all in," said McLinden. "We are making that decision to absorb what he tells us now. There are guys seeking clarity on our game plan whereas they hadn't contributed much before. The results are there for everyone to see over the last couple of weeks."

Going into the Easter weekend, McLinden was confident the recent upturn in form would finally translate into much-needed Super League points. Quins were scheduled to play two games in four days, taking on Catalans Dragons on Good Friday and Wigan Warriors on Easter Monday. Only Wigan lay below them in the table. Yet, on the positive side, Huddersfield Giants, who occupied the last of the play-off spots, were just five points ahead.

Conditions for the visit of the Catalans on 14 April were a world away from those experienced by the Quins players at St Helens. By the time the team emerged from the changing room to go through their pre-match routine at the Stoop, rain had given way to sunshine. There was a relaxed atmosphere around the ground, too, as Easter bunnies dished out chocolate eggs to young and not so young spectators.

Rob Purdham and Zebastian Luisi were both back in the Quins team - a welcome boost given the injury problems so far. Karl Temata, Solomon Haumono and Filomone Lolohea were still missing but homing in on a return to action too. "We've had a bit of bad luck with injuries," said physiotherapist Tim Needham, another Australian. "We've lost a few key guys at the wrong time and players get extremely frustrated watching their team-mates run out for training. Sometimes I feel like half-counsellor, half-physiotherapist because players need to be reassured and encouraged. Thankfully, it's settling down now."

The Catalans arrived in west London in good heart. They had made a positive start to life in Super League and looked far from the whipping boys most people anticipated them to be. Guaranteed their top-flight status for three seasons, they had opened with a shock win over Wigan in the south of France before claiming the scalps of Warrington and Castleford. What's more, they had beaten both the Wolves and the Tigers without the mercurial Stacey Jones. The Golden Boot winner in 2002 had broken an arm against Salford in round two and would also be missing for the game at the Stoop.

Harlequins RL and the Catalans had met in a pre-season friendly in Perpignan. The visitors had come out on top then, winning 46-6, but the Good Friday clash promised to be a lot tighter. Certainly any feeling of solidarity the clubs may have had - after all, they were both battling for acceptance into the Super League fraternity - was cast aside for 80 minutes.

Quins started positively, completing their first set and dominating field position. When they opted to run the ball instead of kicking for goal after being awarded a penalty, they were rewarded with a try from Luisi. The home side extended their advantage when Purdham touched down after Thomas Leuluai's crossfield kick was followed by two good offloads. The Dragons looked to hit back but Quins held out for five consecutive sets. Bruno Verges eventually broke through the Quins line, passing for Sean Rudder to score, but the home side responded, a series of basketball-style passes on the stroke of half-time ending with Luke Dorn going over in the corner. Two brilliant steps from Leuluai after the restart dazzled the Dragons defence and allowed him to stride over for a try under the sticks. Then a brilliant move, involving the sort of free-flowing rugby the club's fans love to see, resulted in Danny Williams going over. Substitute Louie McCarthy-Scarsbrook also got in on the act, scoring his first try for the club as Quins rocketed into a 32-4 lead. Dorn completed the scoring for the home side with a 70-metre intercept try five minutes from time. For all the attractive rugby on display, though, it was a thunderous tackle from Nick Bradley-Qalilawa that best characterised the Quins effort that afternoon. With the home side leading 20-4, the winger flattened opposite number Verges, the collision producing a sickening crunch that resonated around the ground.

With their first league win at the Twickenham Stoop tucked safely under their belts, Harlequins RL headed to Wigan on Easter Monday in high spirits. Normally a trip to the JJB Stadium would have been a pretty daunting proposition but the Warriors were in disarray. With just one win from their eight league games, the once mighty club, who had dominated the British game in the 1980s and early 1990s, had shocked the rugby league world by sacking coach Ian Millward after just 11 months at the helm. The Australian had guided St Helens to every trophy in the book before being sacked for gross misconduct in May 2004, but his proud record counted for little as he struggled to turn around the fortunes of bitter rivals Wigan. He was eventually axed just 72 hours before the club's Good Friday clash with Saints, leaving the Warriors searching for their seventh coach in seven years. Frank Endacott, sacked as Wigan boss in 2001, had said the position had become a "poisoned chalice". But that assessment did not stop a whole raft of top-class candidates being linked with the job. As Quins prepared to head north, the name of Brian Noble was featuring prominently. The Great Britain coach was responsible for guiding Bradford Bulls to five straight Super League Grand Finals, but it appeared all was not well behind the scenes at Odsal. Many doubted Noble would swap Bradford for a club in trouble at the other end of the table. But, as the sacking of both Millward and Hull's John Kear had shown, it was wise to expect the unexpected.

Ian Lenagan, in his programme notes for the match against Catalans, reminded Quins fans that Wigan had been one of the clubs who wanted the Broncos booted out of Super League in March 2005. Lenagan had not been involved with the Broncos then, but he obviously took Wigan's stance very personally. The Wigan-born businessman had retribution on his mind.

It turned out to be a very painful retribution, too. Quins took command from the start, Dorn scoring his side's first try after just three minutes and Matt Gafa crossing again with eight minutes gone. By the break, Quins were 26-8 up, David Mills having scored his first try for the club after a big hit from Joe Mbu had shaken the ball loose from Jordan James. Another bone-crunching tackle on Wigan captain Sean O'Loughlin, this time from Mark Tookey, led to another try for the visitors after the break, rendering the game all but over. Wigan, whose fans had booed them off at half-time, grabbed two tries in consolation, one of them from former Broncos player Dennis Moran, but it was too little too late. Quins, who eventually ran out 30-18 winners, had another two valuable points. Lenagan had his revenge, too.

The Easter performances pleased Tony Rea. After beating the Catalans, he singled out the forwards for special praise and felt that the defence had improved markedly in the last couple of weeks. As for the win over Wigan, he thought that was down to the players' tenacity and desire. "In all my time here I have not seen as much energy in an Easter game," he enthused. "The players didn't care that they had played two days before, that was not even mentioned. It just showed the toughness we had been working on was there."

For Quins fans, two wins in four days was a fantastic and very welcome return. But one supporter was quick to issue a note of caution after the win at the JJB Stadium: "Let's not draw too many conclusions from a solid performance against a demoralised team with no forwards who have probably never coughed up the ball as many times in their lives." He or she may have had a point, but the mood in the Quins camp was on the up.

5. Return of the king

"If they were at Griffin Park, then I may not have come, but they're not. It wasn't part of the choice I had to make."
Henry Paul, Harlequins RL player

Jon Wells ordered a herbal tea and a slice of cake before taking a seat at one of the tables in Emily's, a cafe situated in the heart of Twickenham town centre. His strawberry-blond hair neatly coiffured, he looked in good shape and decent spirits. He certainly did not look like a player who had just got some more bad news on the injury front.

Wells had already spent the best part of six months on the sidelines. Now he was facing another six to eight weeks in the stands after being told the broken metatarsal in his left foot was not healing as well as he had hoped. Instead of stepping up his training in the hope of making the game against Huddersfield on 29 April, he was facing another operation, yet more rehabilitation and a possible return in late June or early July.

Intelligent and eloquent, Wells is not your average rugby league player. He studied law at Leeds University and gained a Masters' degree in criminal justice. Among his numerous interests is landscape photography, which took him and his girlfriend to the west coast of the United States at the end of 2005, to places like San Francisco, Las Vegas and Yosemite National Park. He has also become a regular figure in the commentary box since his injury problems began, providing valuable insights alongside BBC London 94.9 presenter Mark Church. Still, the winger's prolonged absence from the pitch has left him a frustrated man.

It was at the end of the 2005 campaign that Wells first began spending a lot of time in the company of medical consultants. After breaking his nose against Bradford he developed breathing problems, prompting him to go under the knife. It was a routine operation, one that would not hamper his pre-season preparations. But in his first training session back, an unintentional elbow from Zebastian Luisi fractured his jaw. More surgery followed. Then, while he was with the team for a couple of warm-up games in southern France, he developed a stress fracture in the fifth metatarsal in his left foot. It was that last injury, the most innocuous of the lot, which proved the most problematic. "I've been very, very lucky in my career, so I can't really complain," said Wells. "I'm 27 and I've played around 215 first-grade games. That's not bad for someone of my age." But he found it hard keeping his weight in check while he waited for the metatarsal to heal. He was able to work on his upper body, but he was unable to do too much else. "I can swim, but I just can't get too much of a sweat on in the pool," he lamented.

Unlike Paul Sykes, who chose to rehabilitate from his kidney injury back in his home town of Dewsbury, Wells, who also hails from Yorkshire, opted to remain in close contact with the club while his body mended. It helped that he felt very much at home in London. His father hails from Woolwich, so there was a connection with the capital long before he moved to the Broncos for the 2004 season. "My dad always talked about the bright lights and everything the city had to offer," says Wells, who bought a house in Twickenham at the start of 2006 and plans to stick around when his playing days eventually come to an end. It is to be hoped that is a few years off yet, but he is already planning ahead. He used to live with Tulsen Tollett and is still close to his former Broncos team-mate. He would like to follow a similar career path as Tollett too, doing some media work before, as he puts it, getting a "proper job". He does not quite mean it like that, but you feel he would like to make use of the qualifications he worked hard for as a student.

Wells has certainly made a big impact in the short time he has spent in the BBC London 94.9 commentary box on matchdays. He does not get paid for his input, but feels he is somehow contributing to the club by helping to raise its profile. He also believes he can give listeners an insight into life behind the scenes at Harlequins RL, leaving Church, the chief commentator, to focus on the action. "Mark is not going to know what I know from training and playing with the team," says Wells. "It's also very cathartic for me. I don't like sitting and watching games, so this gives me something to do, keeps my mind occupied."

Refusing to sugar-coat what he sees out on the pitch, Wells has won plenty of praise for his honesty. The fans appreciate such an approach, although not everyone is happy. One unidentified critic was less than impressed with his work during the 64-14 defeat at Huddersfield on 19 March, when Wells was particularly critical of the side's performance, lambasting his team-mates for their errors. A few weeks on, Wells remained unrepentant. "You call it how you see it," said the winger, who insisted there has been no backlash from his team-mates. "That's your role as a commentator or summariser. I stand by everything I said."

Church is only too happy to have Wells with him in the commentary box. "I know it has been disappointing for Wellsy being injured for so long but, from my selfish point of view, it has been great to have him alongside me," he says. "He spots things that I never would and knows better than I do what is going on out there in the middle. He also knows what is probably being said in the dressing room before, during and after a game. He's a very good broadcaster and a very intelligent man." As for any criticism that Wells had been too hard on the team, Church insists the player has nothing to apologise for. "Wellsy speaks his mind and that's fair enough," he says. "If you listen carefully, it's clear he cares a lot about Harlequins and wants them to win, but it is very hard when a side is losing badly to be anything but honest. He would be a mug to say there was a chance of the team coming back to win a game when they are 40-0 down at half-time. As for the Huddersfield game, there is no way you can say that was a good performance. You have to call it as you see it."

Harlequins RL had improved from that dismal showing at the Galpharm Stadium, but they were still struggling for consistency. For Wells, who arrived in London at the start of 2004, it was a familiar tale. Just when the club looked as though it might cement itself a place in the top half of the table, it would lose a few games and the spectre of relegation would rear its ugly head again. Still, Wells has no regrets about making the move south. After beginning his career with Castleford, where he spent four years, and then moving to Wakefield for the 2003 season, he felt a switch to the Broncos was just what he needed. It would freshen up his career and give him the chance to develop as a player.

"Tony Rea was known for being a deep thinker, so that attracted me," says Wells, who signed for the club at the end of 2003. "The fact that the club were going to spend 10 weeks in Dubai prior to the start of the season was also a big factor. I thought to myself that I was never going to get that chance in life again. The move offered me lots of other opportunities as well. I saw it as a chance to push for representative honours. After all, I was leaving a team that had finished in 11th place to go to a top-six side. As it turned out, London ended up struggling in my first season and Wakefield made it into the top six."

The Broncos made amends the following year by reaching the play-offs, but in their first season as Harlequins RL things were not going quite to plan. "It's been a very mixed bag and not what we were expecting," said Wells. "I don't think it's going to be a relegation battle but it's going to be a battle to get into the top six. Before the season started, our goal was fourth place, but a lot of the other teams have strengthened while one or two, like Salford, have surprised people. They are playing with confidence, which is something we have lacked. It's very hard to know where our confidence has gone."

Harlequins RL had collected just seven points from their opening 11 games. It was hardly play-off form, though one or two results - like the draw at Odsal and the win at Hull - suggested the team had more to offer. The trouble was, they were losing to sides they expected to beat, like Wakefield and Castleford. Sure, they had showed plenty of guts in the 16-6 defeat at St Helens on 7 April before recording back-to-back wins over Catalans and Wigan, but just when it looked like they were gaining some momentum, they suffered a feeble loss at Wakefield on 23 April. Quins had trailed 24-12 at the break before closing to within two points at the start of the second half. But errors again crept into their game, allowing the Wildcats to run out convincing 42-22 winners.

It was hard for Quins fans not to feel a little uneasy at this point in the season. Their side was neither a strong play-off candidate nor a relegation certainty, yet there was potential for both scenarios to come true. At least the team had an early chance to set the record straight against Huddersfield. Just six weeks after the 64-14 pummelling at the Galpharm Stadium, the Giants were on their way to west London for the return fixture.

The game against Huddersfield on 29 April was more than just a question of setting the record straight, though. Not only was the match being shown live on Sky, it was also the second half of an historic double-header at the Twickenham Stoop. NEC Harlequins would wrap up their promotion-winning campaign back to the top flight by taking on National League One rivals Plymouth Albion at 3pm. Then Harlequins RL would take to the field for their clash with the Giants. It was a deliberate move and a unique opportunity for fans of both union and league to get a taste of the rival code.

Ian Lenagan and Nic Cartwright had long pinpointed the double-header as a major marketing opportunity for the club. They did not need to do much to entice people to buy tickets - the fixture was always going to be a sell out once it became clear NEC Harlequins were destined for an immediate return to the Premiership - but they were still keen to make the clash with Huddersfield a must-see game. To ensure it was, they chose the Thursday before the match to make an announcement that would stun the rugby league world.

Henry Paul is one of rugby league's most decorated players. Born in Tokoroa in New Zealand on 10 February 1974, he has scooped major honours with not one but two clubs - Wigan Warriors and Bradford Bulls - and has set numerous individual records, several of which still stand. He has won Challenge Cups and Super League Grand Finals and has been awarded both the Lance Todd and Harry Sunderland trophies. He has also made 23 international appearances for his native New Zealand. Many felt it was a huge waste of talent when he decided he had had enough of rugby league in November 2001 and switched codes.

Fast forward to April 2006 and Paul is still revered by rugby league fans the length and breadth of the country. However, his feats had been overshadowed somewhat by his failure to set union alight. With seven caps for England - not content with changing codes he had also changed nationality thanks to a grandfather who hailed from Liverpool - he could rightly claim to have been a hit. But so much more had been expected of him. Former Wigan team-mate Jason Robinson had become a union player a year earlier than Paul and had gone on to help England win the World Cup in 2003. Paul was regarded as equally talented, perhaps more so, yet had been unable to establish himself in the England team. He had missed out on the historic triumph in Australia and fallen out of favour with England coach Sir Clive Woodward's successor, Andy Robinson. In fact, Robinson had humiliated Paul by hauling him off after just 16 minutes of a test match against the Wallabies in November 2004. It was a very public fall from grace for the Gloucester player, who was never to play for the England XV-a-side-team again. Instead he became an integral part of the England Sevens set-up, helping the side make its mark in such far-flung and exotic places as Hong Kong and South Africa.

However, sevens rugby was not enough to satiate the 32-year-old Paul, who was itching for another challenge. On 27 April 2006, he decided he had had his fill of union and returned to league. For those who had watched his career closely, it was not a surprise. However, his choice of destination was.

Harlequins RL had been chasing Paul for a while. They began their pursuit in November 2005, keen to sign him before Super League XI began. He had turned down that initial approach, having not yet given up hope of forcing his way back into first-team contention at Gloucester. He was also keen to win a gold medal with the England Sevens team at the Commonwealth Games, which were being held in Melbourne in March.

Unfazed by Paul's rejection, Quins continued to watch his fortunes from a distance, waiting for a sign that he may be about to have a change of heart. Once the Commonwealth Games were over – England won silver in the sevens after falling to New Zealand in the final – and it became increasingly unlikely that Paul would again play a major role at Gloucester, they tried their luck once more. This time, their promptings were rewarded. Several newspapers got wind that Paul was on his way back to league after his four-year sojourn in union, but it was the Australian National Rugby League and Penrith Panthers that looked the likely destination. Harlequins RL did not even register on the radar. Yet on 27 April, the club announced one of the biggest transfer coups in its 26-year history.

The signing of Paul, whose last game of rugby league had been Bradford's Super League Grand Final win over Wigan Warriors in 2001, was big news in its own right, but his move to Harlequins RL took on added significance when it was announced he would play against Huddersfield on 29 April. Not only would his return be screened live by Sky, but lining up for the opposition would be Robbie Paul, his younger brother. It was a marketing man's dream.

Tony Rea was delighted with the capture of Paul. At the press conference to officially unveil him as a Quins player, Rea, whose poker face normally gives little away, could not stop smiling. "It's a really significant signing, not only this season but in the history of the club," he gushed. "What I saw of Henry before he went to rugby union, I always thought he was the most dominant player and the most effective in the competition. He handles the pressure situations so well. I really think he can help this team."

Paul was naturally enthusiastic about the move and said all the things he was expected to say. He praised Ian Lenagan for his progressive thinking and said he looked forward to helping the club make its mark in Super League. He had to deal with the inevitable questions about his time in union, most of which seemed to concentrate on his purported failure to make the grade, but he took them all in his stride. However, his performance was not totally convincing. He let slip that he had wanted to stay put at Gloucester a little longer. More worryingly, he told one journalist that he had been keen on a move to rugby union club Bath, but it had not worked out.

One thing was for certain, Paul would not have entertained the idea of a move to London had the club still been ensconced at Griffin Park. "Maybe not, to be honest," he said. "What was put in front of me and my family was too good to say 'no'. They've got a good squad and a chairman who is really keen to see the club thrive. If they were at Griffin Park, then I may not have come, but they're not. It wasn't part of the choice I had to make."

The majority of Quins fans welcomed the signing of Paul, but there were a few who were a little nervous. Their main fear was that, at 32, he was past his best and not as hungry for success as he once was. It was a legitimate concern, but one he quickly rejected. "I think I can bring a lot of enthusiasm if nothing else," he insisted. "I've come here to win stuff, not just be part of the environment."

If Paul's arrival failed to impress some fans, the same cannot be said of his new team-mates. "Sniffer [Tony Rea] told us there was another player coming and I think everyone expected it to be a loan player just to add to the numbers," said Quins skipper Mark McLinden. "Then we were told it was Henry Paul. We weren't sure

Welcome back Henry Paul

The signing of Henry Paul in April was a major coup for the club. Top: In action against Leeds at Headingley (photo: David Williams); Left: Being interviewed at his first Quins press conference (photo: Philip Gordos); above: With his daughter at the last match of the season. (Photo: Peter Lush)

if Sniffer was joking, but it's good news for the club. I think he fits perfectly with our team."

Chief executive Nic Cartwright was equally bullish about Paul's arrival on a two-and-a-half year contract. The club had spent its transfer budget for the year when it had signed Matt Gafa, but the chance to sign Paul was just too enticing and the board of directors decided to dig a little deeper. "I don't think the owners look at it as breaking the budget," said Cartwright. "We want to grow the club and Henry is a great signing."

Cartwright revealed that Lenagan had played a key role in convincing Paul that his future laid at the Twickenham Stoop. "Ian was very involved," said the club's chief executive. "It's his first real significant contribution to the club and you would struggle to make a better one, short of signing Jonny Wilkinson. Henry's a better player anyway to be honest." Lenagan's first significant contribution was probably agreeing to become joint owner of the club and then chairman, but it is easy to see what Cartwright meant. The recruitment of Paul was a big deal, no matter how you looked at it. But it was also a gamble. Did he still have the necessary desire? Was he fit enough? With the abundance of half-backs already at the club, did they really need another one? Just where did Rea plan to play him? There were also past stories of ill discipline. Paul had been suspended by Gloucester for missing three days of training after attending team-mate Mike Tindall's birthday party.

Paul's arrival at Harlequins RL only heightened the sense of occasion ahead of the double-header on 29 April. The club had already attached huge significance to the game against Huddersfield. After all the talk about a harmonious working relationship with their rugby union cousins, the partnership would finally come under real public scrutiny for the first time. Cartwright, especially, knew that those fans who opposed the link-up with NEC Harlequins would be looking for any hint of discord to justify their well-aired fears that the partnership was ill-thought out and a waste of time and energy.

Cartwright need not have worried. At the end of a perfect sunny day in west London, he was able to sit back and reflect on a job well done. NEC Harlequins had capped their promotion-winning season with a workmanlike 39-15 victory over a gutsy Plymouth Albion side. Then, after the applause and traditional union cries of "heave" had long since died away, Harlequins RL had taken to the field and beaten Huddersfield 22-16.

"We're very happy with how the day went," reflected Cartwright. "We're very happy that we won and because a lot of people watched the game. There was always a concern that the union fans would go off to the bar once their match was over, but a lot of them stayed and they seemed to get into it. All in all, we're happy."

Estimates suggested around half of the 12,000 crowd that had watched the union game had remained in their seats to see Harlequins RL beat Huddersfield. It was clear, too, that the union fans had not stayed just so they could turn their noses up at the rival code. As Michael Aylwin noted in his *Observer* article the next day, "there was a hell of a lot of love coursing through the all-new stadium at the Stoop".

Listen hard enough and the odd partisan comment would have been audible, but that was inevitable. It was more banter than barracking anyway. Take the group of 20-something union fans who were sitting in the North Stand. Midway through the league game, the giant frame of Huddersfield's Eorl Crabtree homed into view. From the relative safety of their seats, they started questioning his sexuality, though never loud enough so he would hear. Had they realised that the long-haired man-mountain was the nephew of Big Daddy, the famous wrestler who lit up British television screens in the 1970s and 1980s, they might well have hit upon something more entertaining to shout.

McLinden was another who caught the eye against Huddersfield. Another dazzling performance from the fleet-footed Australian full-back, who possesses more magic in his feet than Michael Flatley ever did, drew a few covetous glances from NEC Harlequins supporters who wondered if he could be tempted to make the switch to union.

No doubt Dean Richards was one of McLinden's admirers, too. A former England rugby union international, the NEC Harlequins coach had rushed back out to watch the league game after fulfilling his own duties. In fact, so keen was he to see what Quins RL were up to that he got a little annoyed when he was accosted by a group of journalists demanding a quote as he went to take his place in the stand. There was plenty of interest in the rival code from the league boys, too, many of whom had played union as youngsters. Karl Temata, looking very relaxed and casual in black shorts and burgundy polo shirt, stood for several minutes watching the action before heading inside to the changing rooms to prepare for the game against Huddersfield.

Victory over the Giants pleased Rea. It was his side's second successive victory at home and, coming after that dismal defeat at Wakefield, was very welcome. It also ensured both sets of fans had plenty to celebrate in the King's Bar after the action on the pitch had drawn to a close.

"There was a little bit of pressure," conceded Rea. "We knew the union guys would handle themselves well. But we wanted to make sure the party did not go flat. We are pleased to come out on top. Today was about character and toughness."

Most of the post-match chat centred on Henry Paul, who had played his part in the success after starting the game on the bench. He had finally trotted onto the pitch after 35 minutes and was inevitably tackled by brother Robbie when he made his first run. Quins were 12-0 up at that stage. But within two minutes of Paul entering the fray, the Giants had reduced the deficit to six points with a try from Stuart Jones. The gap was down to two just after the interval, when a grubber kick from Robbie eluded his brother, allowing James Evans to score. After Quins made it 16-10 with a try from Nick Bradley-Qalilawa, Crabtree felt it was time to give Paul a proper welcome back. Paul has no doubt received a few facials during his career, but Crabtree's big hands seemed hell bent on rearranging his features, not just giving them a gentle massage.

Paul eventually got on the scoresheet with 10 minutes to go, converting Bradley-Qalilawa's second try of the match. It was third-time lucky for the new recruit, who had missed his first two kicks at goal, but it gave the Quins a decisive 12-point cushion. With three minutes to go, the Giants hit back with a try from Stuart Donlan that Michael De Vere converted. But Quins held on for a much-needed victory.

In a packed media room after the game, Paul, still in his kit but with sandals on his feet instead of boots, lapped up the attention. "I'm bloody knackered now," was his opening comment to the members of the press. He admitted the pace and relentless nature of the game had caught him out, but he thanked his new team-mates for looking after him. "In union, when the ball goes out you walk to a line-out. In league, it's non-stop," he said. "I've got to get used to that. I got lost a couple of times, but I was just really happy that the guys were talking to me the whole game. I think they must have been told in training to keep talking to me – and it worked."

Paul had been anxious to please, aware that any flaws would be exposed by the opposition and flagged up by the fans. "I was just trying to play my part and show the boys that I can still play," he said. "I don't think I missed any tackles and I was happy with my talk. I was trying to encourage the guys around me and they were doing the same for me. We were bouncing off each other."

Now his first match was out of the way, Paul said he was keen to find his best position. He had played at half-back, at centre and at loose-forward during his short time on the pitch against Huddersfield. That is a considerable task for anyone, but it was very impressive for a player who had spent the last five years playing another sport and who had only had time for one training session with his new team. If nothing else, it showed just how highly Rea rated his latest signing.

"I thought he was outstanding," said the Quins coach, who admitted it must have been a bit of a "head spin" for Paul in the 24 hours leading up to the game. After appearing before the media at Friday's press conference and posing for the obligatory photographs in full Harlequins RL kit, he had gone on to complete his all-important medical before heading for what would be a crucial training session with his new team-mates. After the introductions were over, he had been given a quick run through of the tactics and defensive strategy Quins would be employing against Huddersfield before finally getting out onto the pitches at Roehampton Vale. Not content with cramming his head with a whole load of new information, Rea then chose to play him at full-back because McLinden could not train. When it came to the actual match, Paul was thrown on at left centre before being asked to fill a number of other positions, both in the threequarters and in the forwards. "We could not have made it harder for him," said Rea. "But I thought he handled it really well."

Victory over Huddersfield not only gave Paul the perfect start to his Harlequins RL career, it also gave him bragging rights over brother Robbie. But when the younger of the two rugby-playing siblings stuck his head round the door to the media room while the Quins conference was still going on, he found Henry in gracious mood. Robbie, who had clearly expected a verbal bashing, was slightly taken aback. Maybe Henry was too tired from his exertions to indulge in his normal banter with his brother. Maybe he was being humble. Whatever the reason, Henry simply turned to Robbie and urged him to say something. Robbie, with a shrug of his shoulders, responded in typical fashion. "If I'd just beaten you, I'd be bragging," he said.

Encouraging as Henry Paul had been in his first competitive game of rugby league for five years, victory over Huddersfield had not been a one-man show. It had required a big defensive effort from the whole team to keep the Giants at bay.

There were also two highly significant tries for Nick Bradley-Qalilawa. After 20 in 31 appearances in 2005, the winger had gone 12 matches without a touchdown in 2006. Then, no sooner had he got one than he was celebrating another. "I've been copping a fair bit off the guys in training and I've had five or six disallowed in the last couple of weeks, so it's good to get one," said the former Wests Tigers and Manly Sea Eagles player. "When you are a winger, scoring tries is something people measure you by."

Commentators, stadium announcers and sports news readers up and down the land were no doubt grateful Bradley-Qalilawa had not been more prolific in 2006. His name on the scoresheet can cause even the most experienced of radio and television journalists to break out into a cold sweat. The 'Bradley' bit is not a problem, but 'Qalilawa'? You can see the panic in an unsuspecting reporter's face when he scans the teamsheet and sees the Australian's name at number five for Quins. There are several options for the beleaguered hack then. Find someone who knows how 'Qalilawa' is pronounced; make up your own pronunciation and hope no-one notices; or hope he does nothing of note in the game. For the record, 'Qalilawa' is pronounced 'Ka-li-laa-waa'.

Having broken his duck for the season, Bradley-Qalilawa was keen to make up for lost time. He certainly felt he was back to somewhere approaching his best. "I had some injuries in the off-season and the start of the year, so I was a bit disjointed myself," he said. "Certainly the last couple of weeks have been better because I have been on the field and able to train. It helps that the team is getting back to full strength, too, because when you are a winger you finish off moves that others create. Most of the time."

It would take a Herculean effort for Bradley-Qalilawa to add to his tally in Harlequins RL's next game. Next up for a rejuvenated Quins side was Leeds Rhinos, the team that had hammered them 60-0 at the Twickenham Stoop back on 25 March.

6. Microphones and millionaires

"For the first time a London club has put on a suit and tie and is starting to look the part. It is not quite Savile Row at the moment, but it will be."
Mike Stephenson, Sky Sports pundit

Little by little, Harlequins RL were winning over the Broncos fans that had grumbled long and hard into their pints of Greene King, or London Pride when news of the move to the Stoop was first announced. The union-league double-header on 29 April had helped convince a lot of doubters that there was plenty of mileage in the partnership and that it was not a one-sided arrangement purely for the benefit of the union mob. There would always be a small minority of supporters waiting for that 'I-told-you-so' moment, but Nic Cartwright and Ian Lenagan were convinced they were on the right path.

One man who always has a pretty shrewd idea what the majority of fans were thinking is Mark Church. The BBC Radio London reporter was in his fifth season of covering the club and knew, by and large, what made it tick. He sympathised with the supporters – in fact he admired them for the travails they had faced and overcome - but he thought the partnership with NEC Harlequins was manna from heaven. He understood why there was resistance, but he did not think it was deep-rooted. In fact, he thought it would have quickly melted away had Quins rattled off a few victories at the start of the season. "The most important thing is the team out on the pitch," said Church. "If the team is winning, then, as far as the supporters are concerned, nothing else matters, certainly not what the team is called or what the players are wearing." As it was, Harlequins RL had lost more than they had won. From 13 games in both league and cup, they had recorded five victories, seven defeats and one draw. Not good enough for some but not a total disaster either. They were still in touching distance of the play-offs after all.

A complete rugby league novice when he began covering the Broncos, Church had quickly earned the respect of the players and fans with both his willingness to learn and obvious enthusiasm for the game. "I knew very little about rugby league before taking on the Broncos, so I got clued up by watching a stack of old videos," he said. "I was quite nervous when I started off. I turned up to training to interview the players and I didn't know anybody. But Scott Cram took me under his wing and made me feel so welcome.

He introduced me to everybody. Now the players are used to me being about the place."

Church quickly became a big fan of the game too. It may have been his job to follow London's fortunes, but he found little hardship in traipsing around the country, reporting from such places as Widnes, Wigan and Warrington. "If I wasn't commentating on the Quins, I'd be turning up to watch them anyway," he said. "It's in my blood now."

A former public schoolboy from Kent who possesses a degree in politics from Durham University and an accent more Eton than Wakefield, Church is not what you might call true rugby league stock. In fact, his style is more Henry Blofeld than Eddie Waring. "Danny Kelly, my colleague at BBC Radio London, thinks I report on games wearing a purple smoking jacket with a glass of Beaujolais in one hand and the microphone in the other," says Church.

Thirty-something Church began his media career with his university radio station but took a job in advertising when he left college. He hated it and decided to enrol on a postgraduate course in journalism at Portsmouth. A job with BBC Southern Counties followed, his beat including both football and cricket. Then he moved to London. His career was beginning to take off when he was forced to have surgery on a back complaint that had steadily worsened from his teenage years. When he eventually made it back onto his feet after spending almost nine months lying rigid in bed, the opportunity to follow the fortunes of the Broncos came his way in May 2002. Needless to say, he grabbed it. "It was completely different to anything I had done before," he said. "But I put the effort in and worked really hard at it. I can remember my dad asking me what I was doing commentating on rugby league but now he's been to every Super League ground. As for my mum, she listens to my commentaries but hasn't got a clue what's going on. She gets very excited, though, when Harlequins win."

The relationship between Church and the club has been a fruitful and rewarding one. For Church, it has been a real adventure following the club around the country, experiencing the same highs, lows and prejudices that the players and fans have faced down the years. As for the club, it has benefited immeasurably from the publicity and support offered to it by its local BBC radio station. Five years ago there were no match commentaries on the airwaves, just a 40-second segment whenever station bosses decided there was space. Now Church reports on every game from every conceivable venue, whether it takes place on a Friday night, Saturday evening or Sunday afternoon.

There is also BBC Radio London's weekly 30-minute show on a Thursday night which gives the club more exposure and the fans the chance to vent their spleen. Church loves the interaction with supporters. As any good journalist should, he has developed a pretty thick hide that protects him from any criticism that comes his way. "If the fans want to send bullets at me, they can," he said. "I don't mind." He particularly loves matchdays, though, when he gets to pour his heart and soul into his commentaries. "I always think about those people who may be listening for the first time," he told us. "We've had calls and emails from people who say they had no idea what was going on but it sounded fantastic and they will definitely be tuning in next time."

According to Church, between 1,500 and 3,000 people listen to his match commentaries. The internet plays its part in those broadcasts, allowing people all over the world to follow the action. "Matt Gafa's uncle, Luke Dorn's father and Karl Temata's family all listen in," said Church. "We know they do because we get emails from them."

Ask any reporter who covers a club week-in week-out and they will tell you it can be hard staying emotionally detached. Inevitably, his or her fortunes are tied to that of the club. Church is no different. "I'm biased, I admit it," he said. "I love it when we win. I've been on my feet cheering after a victory. On the flip side, when we've lost I've sat there with my head in my hands after the final hooter has sounded. That's the great thing about this club. They win when you think they are going to lose and lose when you expect them to win. But at least they keep us on our toes."

Yet this is not simply a job for him. Church has forged some kind of bond with the club in the last five years. He found out just how deeply he had become attached on 4 March 2005, when the Broncos came within a whisker of losing their Super League status.

"After all they had been through, I was thinking it would be such a shame to see them go now," said Church, casting his mind back to that eventful Friday in Huddersfield. "I would have been gutted. I wasn't entirely sure what was going on, all the ins and outs, but I knew they were in the mire financially. I remember going to my office and telling everyone that the club could be on its way out. I didn't know what to think, but Nic Cartwright had told me he would call when the meeting was over. He eventually phoned around 5pm and told me the good news, that the club was safe. But he also said it had been a close call, that at one point he thought the club was dead."

Harlequins RL have other friends in the media besides Church. *The Guardian's* Andy Wilson has written several favourable articles, as has Dave Hadfield of *The Independent*. What's strange is that the main London newspaper, the *Evening Standard*, almost ignores the club. The *Metro*, the London morning free sheet, often devotes a page or two to the club and rugby league in general, but not the *Standard*.

One man who takes every opportunity to champion London's cause is Sky Sports pundit Mike 'Stevo' Stephenson. Maybe it's because he lives in the capital and is keen for the game to flourish there that he is so vocal. Maybe it's because the former Great Britain captain is mates with both Ian Lenagan and David Hughes. In fact, it was Stephenson who was responsible for Lenagan taking more than a passing interest in the club in 2005.

Sitting in a pub near London Bridge with a glass of wine in front of him, Stephenson reluctantly shed some light on his involvement in the deal that brought Lenagan to the club. "I'd known Ian for a few years," he explained. "He started off as an acquaintance but now we're good friends. I remember being invited to speak at a pre-match dinner at the Oxford and Cambridge Varsity game at Richmond a couple of years ago. Afterwards Ian bought me a drink and quickly turned the conversation to rugby league and its future. He agreed with some of what I said and disagreed with other bits, but I got the impression he thought rugby league wasn't going in the way he thought possible. Here was a man who knew a lot about the game and who had a lot of opinions about how it could be improved. Some were radical, but it was clear he was passionate. So when the Broncos were nearly booted out of Super League, I called him up and asked him if he wanted to get involved with the club."

Stephenson thought Lenagan's business brain and money would be a real asset to the Broncos. He also felt it was time David Hughes was given a much-needed helping hand in his one-man quest to keep the club afloat.

"David was a brave man to take over from Richard Branson," said Stephenson. "If Branson couldn't make it work, then who could? I think most people thought David was chasing fool's gold, but he was determined, a battler who was happy taking on the big boys. But no one, even someone who has done well in business, can afford to keep throwing money away. You had to admire him for what he'd done, which is why I was so disappointed that they'd nearly been booted out. The morning after the meeting in Huddersfield, I rang David and told him I thought it would be a good idea if he had someone alongside him to share the workload and especially some of the financial responsibility. He liked the idea, so I told him I had a friend who was as mad about rugby league as he was and arranged a meeting."

Stephenson was present for most of the negotiations between Lenagan and Hughes, recalling quite clearly the day they finally

Salloos restaurant – the venue for a key meal in the club's future.
(Photo: Philip Gordos)

cemented their partnership. The three of them met at a Pakistani restaurant, Salloos, in Knightsbridge, an upmarket district in central London. Stephenson cannot recall what the others had to eat, but he remembers tucking into a chicken vindaloo. His hunger satiated and the talks gathering pace, Stephenson eventually made his excuses and left, preferring not to be party to any discussions concerning finance. But he did not head home. He crossed the road and took up residence at the bar of the Wilton Arms, where he had agreed to meet Lenagan and Hughes after they had finished talking. "When they came in, I asked them if they had done a deal, and they said 'yes'," recalled Stephenson. "We celebrated, but there was no champagne, not for these two guys. They may be millionaires, but they wanted nothing more than a pint of bitter each. As for me, I had a magnificent glass of sauvignon blanc."

Stephenson had no doubt Lenagan would breathe new life into the Broncos. When the club subsequently announced it would be forming an alliance with NEC Harlequins, his optimism only increased. Not everyone shared his view, though. Within hours of the partnership becoming public knowledge, Stephenson received several irate calls from NEC Harlequins friends deeply disturbed at the prospect of slumming it with league. One conversation in particular stuck in Stephenson's mind.

"I had a call from a friend of mine who is a High Court Judge," said Stephenson. "He wasn't very happy and bellowed in my ear, 'How could this happen, why wasn't I told?' I started laughing, but he carried on complaining. I tried to explain that it was a move that would benefit both sides, but he wasn't having any of it."

Like a lot of people, Stephenson thinks the move to the Stoop could be the start of something big for Harlequins RL. Or in his words: "For the first time a London club has put on a suit and tie and is starting to look the part. It is not quite Savile Row at the moment, but it will be." He also has a theory over why some fans refuse to embrace the new venture, particularly those who have supported the club from the very start. "They have become quite possessive of the club after going through all the trials and tribulations and near-death experiences," said Stephenson, who clearly fancies himself as an amateur psychologist. "If crowds do go up to 6,000, 7,000 or 8,000, then they will lose that exclusivity. It won't be their little club anymore. That's why there is resentment."

Let's get one thing straight here. The Mike Stephenson we spoke to was very different to the Stevo you see on Sky Sports each week. He is paid to be outspoken on television, to say things that engender a reaction. He doesn't suddenly become mute when he is away from the cameras, but he no longer has to play to an audience either.

Stephenson's opinions are clearly valued by Hughes and Lenagan, whatever fans may think. He often acts as a sounding board for both men, particularly when big decisions are pending. For example, he told them they were taking a risk by signing Henry Paul. "It was a very brave move," said Stephenson. "However, irrespective of his age and the amount of time he has been out of rugby league, his signing showed to everyone the club is thinking big and trying to build a quality side."

If Harlequins RL are to take some giant strides towards enticing more Englishmen to the Stoop, then it is about creating a winning team on the pitch, not just about what the city of London has to offer. Stephenson thinks more significant signings could be on their way, too. Maybe even a big-name English recruit. "There is still this fear factor in the north of England that London is the most unkind place in the world," said Stephenson. "They have this perception, still, that Londoners think of them as wearing flat caps with a whippet under one arm. It's ludicrous. London is a great city, it's full of history, and it has a lot to offer everyone, including families."

Stephenson is biased, of course, but he goes on to make an important point. "Most fans in the north think nothing of flying to Greece or Spain and know how to order a beer when they get there," said Stephenson. "Yet they are either afraid or find it irritating to make the short trip to London. Some clubs have taken more fans to Perpignan than to the Stoop. We have got to get the message across that London is a great place to come to. People who make the trip from places like Leeds, Bradford, Warrington or wherever have got to spread the gospel. London is wonderful."

The victory over Huddersfield had given the club a big lift, but now they faced two massive fixtures against Leeds and Bradford, two giants of the modern game. Win one of those and the momentum would really swing their way as they looked to achieve their goal of making the play-offs.

The players and coach were upbeat, but the trip to Headingley did not engender too much optimism amongst the fans. The Rhinos had romped to a 60-0 win at the Stoop six weeks previously and were riding high near the top of the table. Quins had upset the odds at Odsal and the Kingston Communications Stadium earlier in the season, but this was a different proposition entirely, plus the team were still dogged by inconsistency. They had enjoyed a pretty profitable April, winning three out of five Super League games and also beating Toulouse in the Challenge Cup. But what would May bring?

Any signs of vulnerability Leeds had shown in losing 44-16 to Warrington the week before were quickly eradicated at Headingley on 5 May. The early exchanges were fairly even, but the Rhinos soon exploded into life. By the 50th minute they had opened up a 30-6 lead over Harlequins RL, with stand-off Danny McGuire inevitably among the try scorers. With Thomas Leuluai on international duty with New Zealand, Quins coach Tony Rea had opted to play Henry Paul from the start alongside Luke Dorn. It was a big ask, but Paul responded to the challenge, although he was powerless to stop the home side from controlling the game. Quins finished the game with a flourish, Mark McLinden adding a second try to the one he scored earlier in the match and Dorn also crossing. But it was not enough. A 36-24 loss suggested a tight game. It was anything but.

Harlequins RL dropped to ninth in the Super League table after the defeat at Leeds, with just nine points from 13 games. Wakefield, the Catalans and Wigan remained below them, but Castleford were up to eighth after their 30-24 win at the JJB Stadium. It was a precarious position for Quins, but there did not seem any reason to panic while Wigan were still rooted to the foot of the table. Despite the appointment of Brian Noble as coach, the Warriors were showing few signs of recovery. They had beaten Huddersfield in his first game, but had then slipped to defeats against Hull FC and now Castleford. It would get worse before it got better, too. Four more defeats would follow, including what looked to be a fatal 10-8 loss against fellow strugglers Wakefield.

Next up after the visit to Leeds was a home game against Bradford on FA Cup final day. There had been speculation that the time of kick-off would be moved back to avoid clashing with football's showpiece occasion. Given that chief executive Nic Cartwright is a West Ham fan, one of the finalists, the rumour gained added credence. But it proved to be wide of the mark.

The Bulls were now led by Steve McNamara following Noble's move to Wigan and had lost two of their three games with the former assistant coach in charge. Quins sensed an upset, but hopes of another win at the Stoop were ruthlessly dashed by half-time, just as West Ham's hopes of a Cup win at Cardiff's Millennium Stadium were cruelly crushed by Liverpool's inspirational captain Steven Gerrard. Five tries in just 15 first-half minutes ended the match as a contest and left Rea sifting through the wreckage of a 58-16 defeat for reasons to be optimistic.

The Quins fans were beginning to get restless, too. They were no longer preoccupied with the club's name change and the move to The Twickenham Stoop. What was focusing their minds was the team's inability to string some decent performances together. They had witnessed two wins in a row only once and they were starting to abandon all hopes of a play-off place. Worse, they were beginning to grow more frustrated with Rea. Had he lost his ability to motivate the team? Were his pre-season signings up to the mark? Why did the team give away so many penalties? And why was the defence so solid one week but so porous the next?

The subject of Rea split fans right down the middle. His backers felt he was the reason the club was still in Super League. He had, they said, an uncanny knack of gelling a side together in a short space of time after the annual exodus of players at the end of each season. He had an eye for talent, he was loyal and he was honest too. Sure, the club was struggling now, but who wouldn't when a growing list of injuries was playing havoc with team selection? Paul Sykes was out for the season, Jon Wells still had not played in 2006 while McLinden had missed the opening weeks of the campaign. Whenever someone was given the all-clear to return, another inevitably headed for the treatment room, like Leuluai, who would be sidelined for the next seven weeks after tearing a hamstring playing for New Zealand.

Rea's critics felt he was only in the job because he was such good mates with joint owner and former chairman Hughes. Rea may have taken the club into the play-offs twice, but it was only a brief flirtation with the top six. One good year was inevitably followed by a poor one. Injuries were no doubt a concern, but then every team had players out. Rea, in their view, was living on borrowed time.

According to Cartwright, speculation about Rea's future was nothing new. It had become a common theme. In any case, many supporters, even those who thought a change was needed, felt sacking Rea at this point would be the wrong thing to do. The club had already experienced a lot of upheaval in a short space of time. Getting rid of the coach would only add to the state of flux. But there were those who thought it was the perfect time for a change of leadership. With Ian Millward and John Kear still out of work, there were a lot of fans who felt the club could afford to be bold and make a change. The name of Rohan Smith was also mentioned. Wasn't he being groomed to take over? At 25, surely it was too early for him to be given such a massive task?

Rohan Smith certainly had the right pedigree. The son of former Bradford Bulls and Hull FC coach Brian Smith and the nephew of current Leeds Rhinos boss Tony Smith, coaching certainly seemed to be in his blood. But then that is no guarantee of success. However, Rohan had already started making waves in the coaching world long before he upped sticks and became part of the Broncos staff in July 2004.

Smith had tried to make it as a player but had failed to reach the grade. A second shoulder reconstruction at the age of 20 eventually put paid to any lingering hopes he may have had, but he had already begun turning his attention to coaching. He became an assistant at Collegians, one of his local sides in Wollongong, and was given responsibility for conditioning, making sure the players were in the best possible shape before they took to the field. For Smith, it seemed like the natural step.

"When I was little I would watch games with my dad and my uncle and was pretty outspoken," he said. "If a player wasn't any good, I said so. If the team was playing badly, I would say they should be doing this or that. My thoughts just came out and would prompt some sort of debate. I may have been only 12 but I guess whatever we talked about helped with the analytical side of things. I was surrounded by the game and forever analysing. I now look at games in more depth. If it's a good game, I want to know why. If someone scores a try, I want to know how it happened."

Smith graduated from the University of Wollongong with a degree in exercise science and nutrition in 2002. His coaching career had also moved on by that stage. While a student, he had started doing some voluntary work for the New Zealand Warriors National Rugby League side coached by Daniel Anderson, who had been his dad's assistant at Parramatta Eels. Smith's job was to watch tapes of matches and make notes, highlighting key incidents so that when Anderson sat down to watch a re-run of a game he had all the necessary information in front of him. "I must have done a reasonable job because he asked me to do it for a second year," said Smith.

Smith was not getting paid for doing what he did but, he says, cash was not an issue. "It was about experience and getting a foot in the door," said Smith. His plan paid off. In December 2002, he received a call from Anderson asking him to come and work full-time for the Warriors. It was the break Smith had been looking for, so he left home and headed for Auckland.

"I went there thinking that I knew a fair bit, but I got a quick shock and learnt a massive amount under Daniel," said Smith, who has nothing but praise for the way Anderson treated him and helped bring him on as a coach. "Some coaches try to keep a lot of things to themselves and don't try to develop the staff around them, but I could tell that he wanted me to progress."

As a high performance analyst, Smith spent a lot of time working with the younger kids as well as helping prepare the senior side. A certain Thomas Leuluai, then 17, was just starting to make a name for himself. A year later, Leuluai was playing a starring role in New Zealand's shock 30-16 win over Australia in Auckland. It was the teenager's international debut and instantly marked him down as a star of the future.

Smith had been part of the New Zealand effort that day, too. With Anderson being both coach of the Warriors and the national team, it was only natural that the young Australian had been recruited to help plot the downfall of his homeland. "That was a big result for league in New Zealand, it really got it pumping a bit," said Smith. He also helped prepare New Zealand for the Anzac test in June the following year and was part of the tour party that travelled to England for the culmination of the Tri-Nations series at the end of 2004. "It was great working with a group of guys at the top of the tree," said Smith. "It was really exciting, if daunting at the same time." He was at London by that stage having left the Warriors in June after Anderson resigned following a poor start to the season. Anderson remained in charge of the Kiwis, only stepping down after agreeing to succeed Ian Millward at Super League club St Helens in May 2005.

Smith had gone back to Wollongong to get a job after leaving the Warriors but was told there was a possible opening with the Broncos, who were without an assistant coach. A few phone calls later, Smith was back in gainful employment. "I had never met Tony Rea before but a few people he knows well and trusts spoke to him," said Smith. "Basically he checked up on me before deciding he wanted me alongside him."

Having spent a few years as a kid in England thanks to his dad's work with Hull FC and Bradford, Smith did not feel like a fish out of water when he arrived in the capital. His age was not an issue either. In fact, he insists his age has never been a problem, though he admits he was not completely comfortable at first giving orders to players, some of whom were 10 years older and vastly more experienced.

"It was pretty daunting to start with, particularly when I was at the Warriors," says Smith, who turned 25 on 5 May 2006. "But most of my hands-on stuff involved the goalkickers and little side projects with blokes that had to improve in certain areas. As long as the players know you are trying to help them and have respect for them I don't think it matters that they have more experience. It doesn't really matter if they are a lot older either. For the first few months I don't think anyone even asked me how old I was. When someone did, it never seemed a problem. Maybe it was for some blokes, but it has never surfaced as an issue. I tend to keep my distance from players anyway. With the responsibility that I have here in London, I have to set an example. The time I spend working means that I'm not into socialising in a big way anyway."

Smith has no idea how many hours he works a week. He cannot actually remember the last day he didn't work. "I never really worry about a day off – I don't really like them," he said. "I feel as though I lose track a little bit."

Smith's main task concerns video analysis. He generally watches a match three times. The first time he will usually watch it straight through at normal speed. The second time he starts making notes, going through the game with a fine toothcomb. Finally he watches it for a third time to gauge the ebbs and flows, where it was won and lost. All the matches are downloaded on to his laptop computer, sometimes as they are taking place, so that when a game is over he can start his work immediately.

When Smith has completed his analysis, the players sit down in front of a big screen in one of the rooms at the Roehampton Vale training ground and given a private showing. If Quins have won, it is a relatively painless experience. If Quins have lost, the last thing a player wants to be shown is how he messed up.

"I think that I was pretty naive when I started," says Smith. "I thought that players would listen because it was their job to and would say if they did not understand something. But I have realised that it is not always as simple as that. It is up to the coaches to ensure a player takes in as much information as possible, so it's important to mix sessions up so they are not always the same, to vary the length and style of presentation, and to make sure the players contribute, whether it's out on the field or in the video room. I remember when I was at school. If the teacher did the same things all the time, the switch went off after about two minutes. It's the same here. If you are speaking to a large group of young men, not all of them will be concentrating. So I try to be as brief and concise as possible."

Smith is also responsible for the defensive strategy that Quins adopt on a week-to-week basis. It is his job to analyse the opposition's attack and come up with a plan to stifle it. "If you put a system together, it is important to stick to it and work hard on it," he says. "Some sides adopt the rush defence, while others use the slide or wedge. I don't tend to use any of those by themselves because at any given time during a game you have to be able to use each of them. If you cannot adapt, then I think you are limited to what you can defend against. Some teams do stick to one system, but that gives you something to attack. Salford, for example, just slide and are very good at it, but there aren't too many in Super League who just do one thing. Most teams can do a bit of each. Here at Quins, we try to defend a bit wider and to put as many scenarios together as possible so players can make a decision whether they need to slide or wedge."

Whatever system Quins use, communication is key, says Smith. "If you don't communicate in defence it does not matter what system you use. We have been improving our communication, but we have still got a way to go. It is tough at times when you are under pressure, but you still have to be able to make a decision."

It is hard to believe that Smith is only 25. Mature, level-headed and a deep thinker, he has made massive strides in just a short time. Whether he fulfils his dream of becoming a head coach in his own right remains to be seen, but he has made a great start.

"I think back to when I began and how much I have progressed, how much more I know, how much more confident I am," he says. "The ultimate for me is to be a head coach in the NRL, but it would be a great honour to coach in Super League too."

7. Young guns having some fun

"We lived together in a house on Beverley Road, one of the main drinking roads in Hull, so naturally we had some fun. It was a big learning curve for us."
Michael Worrincy, Harlequins RL player

The fifth-round draw of the Powergen Challenge Cup paired Harlequins RL with National League 2 side Barrow Raiders. It was a gift. Even on a bad day and without Henry Paul, who was ineligible, because he had not signed in time, Quins would surely have enough firepower to see off the part-timers from Cumbria. So it proved. Roared on by an extremely vocal band of 100 fans, Barrow showed plenty of pluck, and in forward Brett McDermott they possessed a player who could match the physical presence of a David Mills or a Danny Williams, but they were no match for a Super League side making the most of the chance to put the boot into lower league opposition.

Several club records fell or were equalled on 20 May as Quins ran in 14 tries in an emphatic 82-8 victory at The Stoop. Rob Purdham set two of them. His individual haul of 34 points broke Greg Barwick's tally of 28, set against Castleford in August 1996, while his 13 goals was one more than Paul Sykes kicked against Wakefield in February 2005. The 82 points Quins put past Barrow also equalled the 82 they had scored without reply against Regal Trophy opponents Highfield at Barnet Copthall in November 1995.

"We played alright but they gave us a game for 20 minutes of each half and I'm sure a few of the boys will be sore because there were a few big hits coming in," said Purdham. "McDermott can tackle, I know him because we played for Cumbria together. He is a real good defender. But there is still a lot of improving for us to do. I thought we were shabby in patches. We dropped balls and came up with some nothing plays that didn't really do anything for us. Our shape off the ball wasn't good at times either. We have to cut out the lapses and be more consistent on the field."

Purdham was quick to play down his record-breaking exploits. "The kicks were mainly easy ones, but I suppose they all have to be converted," said the former Whitehaven player who had started the season as third-choice goalkicker behind Sykes and Matt Gafa. "I just keep practising in case someone gets injured and I get a go. Today I did." Tony Rea disagreed with Purdham's modest assessment. "It wasn't only his points, his touches looked really strong as well and I was impressed with him in sight of traffic," said the Quins coach, who had watched Barrow play a league game against London Skolars a couple of weeks previously. "We thought he had broken his hand last week, so to see him come out and play so strongly was a tremendous twist in our week."

Still, the victory had only come at the expense of part-time National League opposition. As Barrow coach Paul Crarey put it: "There is a massive gulf between our level and Super League. Quins had too much power and pace for us. They ripped us apart around the rucks."

With a place in the Challenge Cup quarter-finals secured, Quins were able to concentrate on improving their league position. The defeats against Leeds and Bradford had dented the team's ever fluctuating confidence levels and left them down in ninth place. It was not panic stations just yet, but they needed a win – and soon. The trip to Salford on 29 May, a Bank Holiday Monday, represented a decent opportunity to get the victory they desperately craved. But the Reds would not be pushovers. They had astounded everyone with their blistering start to the season, winning eight of their 14 games to lie sixth. They had been as high as third after nine rounds, accumulating seven wins to lie behind only St Helens and Leeds, but their form had dipped of late. Still, they were a formidable force, boasting players of the calibre of Luke Robinson, Andrew Dunemann, Malcolm Alker, David Hodgson and Simon Finnigan, who was scoring tries for fun from loose-forward.

As expected, the game swung one way and then the other as both sides mixed attacking creativity with some shoddy defending. At half-time, Quins led 18-12 thanks to tries from Danny Williams, Lee Hopkins and Solomon Haumono. But Salford hit back and looked to have taken control of the game when tries from Ian Sibbit and Stuart Littler, his third of the game, put them 22-18 up. With 14 minutes to go, Michael Worrincy's incisive break led to Mark McLinden, who had signed a new three-year contract in the run-up to the game, touching down in the right-hand corner. This levelled the scores, but a Gareth Haggerty try five minutes from time looked to have sealed the win for the home side. Again Quins stormed back, this time Pat Weisner diving over after another memorable Worrincy burst. Then, with the scores locked at 28-28 and with 30 seconds left, Henry Paul, making only his fourth appearance in a Quins shirt, landed a match-winning drop-goal from 40 metres out. As the kick sailed through the posts, Paul sprinted back into his own half, refusing to celebrate and urging his team-mates to stay completely focused for the final few seconds. Only when referee Richard Silverwood finally blew for full-time did Quins allow their guard to drop. Paul was mobbed by his entire team as the Salford players stood shell-shocked, unable to comprehend what had happened. The Quins fans who had made the trip to The Willows could not believe their eyes either. Leaping up and down on the terraces, they realised they had witnessed something special. As usual Williams was one of the first players across to applaud the supporters who had made the trek north. But he was quickly joined by the rest of the team.

The win, only their fourth in the league, moved Quins up three places to eighth in Super League, five points behind Salford in sixth. It was a massive lift. Rea was ebullient and naturally singled out Paul for praise. "When it gets tough, Henry likes to throw his hand up," he said. "His class was a big factor." Paul played down his role in the win. "I didn't think we'd get a chance for a late drop-goal but when I got the ball I just put my head down and swung," he said. It was a typically modest claim.

Henry Paul duly grabbed the newspaper headlines after the dramatic win over Salford, but it was the display of Michael Worrincy that had most Quins fans salivating. He had scored a try and set up two more, causing the Reds all sorts of problems with his power, agility and sheer youthful exuberance. Just when the home side thought they had shackled him, he would get his legs pumping again, like pistons on a steam engine, and players would drop off him like leaves on a tree.

Worrincy, a 20-year-old loose-forward, had made his senior debut just a fortnight before, in the home hammering by Bradford on 13 May, and had done enough to retain his place in the side for the record-breaking Challenge Cup win over Barrow the following week. Now here he was against Super League opposition leaving no-one in any doubt that he was a potential star of the future.

Born in Leeds, Worrincy came to London in the early 1990s. A keen footballer, he was persuaded to try his luck at rugby league by Stuart Hogg, one of his teachers at St Joseph's Academy in Lewisham. "Mr Hogg used to spend some lunch hours watching re-runs of State of Origin games and we used to take a look, too," explained Worrincy, who attended St Joseph's with elder brother Rob and Quins team-mate Louie McCarthy-Scarsbrook. "We saw people smashing into each other and thought we'd like a bit of that."

Worrincy proved to be pretty adept at a sport that was still developing in London. He quickly made his mark at amateur side Greenwich Admirals and soon came to the attention of the London Broncos. He captained their junior academy team in 2004 and ended up catching the eye of the BARLA selectors, who named him in their under-18 squad for the tour of Australia at the end of the

Barrow thrashed as records tumble

Quins showed no mercy against their National League 2 opponents

Celebrating another Quins try. The home side scored 14 tries in their 82-8 victory, a club record.
(Photos: Peter Lush).

Michael Worrincy, in only his second senior game for Quins, scored a brace of tries against the Raiders.

The thumping of Barrow set up a quarter final with Leeds Rhinos.

Rob Purdham kicks through – his two tries and 13 goals set a new club record 34 points in a match.
(All photos: Peter Lush)

year. But with the Broncos still without a senior academy side, Worrincy found himself being loaned out to a rival Super League club for the 2005 season. The move to Hull FC proved a highly significant one, not just for Worrincy but fellow Broncos youngsters Louie McCarthy-Scarsbrook, Ade Adebisi and Ian Lane. Here were four cocky kids from London looking to make their mark in a city that lived and breathed rugby league. It was a big ask, but they wasted little time in proving they were there on merit. Not only did they win respect for their talent and attitude, they helped Hull win the Senior Academy Grand Final, a massive achievement.

"We knew it would be hard but we held our own," said Worrincy. "There were times when we wondered what we were doing up there, but we were confident in our ability. It helped that people were very open with us. We made some good friends and we sometimes got recognised when we were out and about. We had a good time. We lived together in a house on Beverley Road, one of the main drinking roads in Hull, so naturally we had some fun. It was a big learning curve for us."

With a sister in Leeds and elder brother Rob playing his rugby league for Sheffield Eagles, Worrincy did not find it hard to settle in East Yorkshire. In fact, he enjoyed life so much he stayed when his commitments to Hull had ended and began playing some games for Batley in the National League. He quickly developed affection for his new team - an affection which was reciprocated. In fact, so enamoured were the Bulldogs that they tried to sign him, and they very nearly succeeded. "The big derby with Dewsbury was coming up and Batley wanted to sign me," said Worrincy. "I'd heard nothing from London, so I thought it would be a good move for me. Then I got a call from Tony Rea. He said I could do better than Batley and wanted me to come back to London. I was in two minds. I didn't want to return to London unless I was going to get an opportunity to prove myself. After a lot of thought, I decided to come back to London and give it a go."

Worrincy had suffered from an attack of nerves before his Super League debut against the Bulls. "I was as nervous as hell, but when I got out there I didn't feel anything," said Worrincy, who lists Ellery Hanley, Joe Lydon, Garry Schofield and Roy Powell among his rugby league heroes. "My team-mates helped me a lot. Danny Williams is a real inspiration while Lee Hopkins told me to just keep on doing what I was good at and keep believing in myself. But I'm still learning and still raw. I'm not going to let anything go to my head." Worrincy had begun the game against the Bulls on the bench but a week later, the second-row forward made the starting line-up for the Challenge Cup tie with Barrow, scoring two tries in the record-breaking victory.

Rea clearly recognised Worrincy's potential. More importantly perhaps, the coach recognised the effect Worrincy had on the Quins fans. "One thing you do notice is the atmosphere when he touches the ball," said Rea. "The Londoners really enjoy the fact the club is putting some effort into producing players." Worrincy may not have been born in the capital, but he is still regarded as a local lad by fans – and there is nothing fans like more than seeing one of their own out there representing their team. Joe Mbu had been the lone standard bearer for several seasons, although he had been born in Africa. But now there was a host of youngsters coming through the ranks, much to the delight of the supporters. Worrincy was one of them, but there was Tony Clubb and Louie McCarthy-Scarsbrook, too.

Clubb had made the first breakthrough, earning an unexpected call-up for the club's second match of the 2006 season, the game at Bradford on 18 February, after impressing in the warm-up games in France and Leeds. "I wasn't expecting to play," recalled Clubb. "I'd gone back to my parents in Gravesend when I got a call at 11pm on Friday telling me I was needed because Luke Dorn was out with a hamstring strain. I had to get up at 5am the next day to catch a train to Leeds. Team manager Dom Fenton met me at the station and took me to the team's hotel so I could get a couple of hours sleep. When I woke up, I was told I was in the 17."

Clubb, who can play at centre or on the wing, did not look out of place as he helped Quins draw at Odsal. But hadn't he been nervous, coming up against the likes of Marcus Bai and Shontayne Hape? "I didn't have a chance to think," said Clubb, who began the game on the bench. "It was all a bit of a whirlwind for me."

Clubb's rise was meteoric for a player who had come late to the game. He had begun his rugby career with union side Blackheath and had ironically turned down the chance of a trial with NEC Harlequins as a 15-year-old. Like Worrincy and McCarthy-Scarsbrook, he was introduced to league at Greenwich Admirals, quickly coming to the attention of the Broncos. Then, after being named junior academy player of the year for the second consecutive time, he was offered the chance to accompany the first team on the pre-season tour to the south of France. That is when he really came to the fore.

Having impressed against Bradford, Clubb started the next game against Wakefield but was undone by opposite number Semi Tadulala as the Wildcats scored a shock success at the Twickenham Stoop. The 18-year-old was left out of the side for trip to Hull but scored his first senior try in the subsequent game against Castleford. Three more followed in the Challenge Cup win over Toulouse, by which time it was clear Quins had unearthed another potential star. By May Clubb was in possession of a new, two-year contract taking him up the end of the 2007 season. "I didn't have an agent, so I talked to Danny Williams and he helped me out," said Clubb. "I wasn't happy with certain things, so Danny told me to make sure I told the club. I ended up getting a good deal."

Williams is one of a number of senior players that the Quins youngsters look up to. "He has done everything in the game, including winning a Grand Final in Australia," said McCarthy-Scarsbrook. "He's 33 and still hungry, still putting the big shots in. He's awesome." Clubb agreed. "He gets everyone going," he said. "So do the others, like Solomon Haumono, Joe Mbu and Lee Hopkins. They lead by example. That's why we look up to them."

Joe Mbu knows what it is like to be a Londoner trying to make his mark at the club. Born in Zaire, now the Democratic Republic of Congo, but brought up in Tottenham, he carried the weight of local expectation for three seasons before the emergence of Clubb, Worrincy and McCarthy-Scarsbrook. Having begun his career with the London Skolars, Mbu also spent a year on loan at both Leeds Rhinos and Huddersfield Giants before breaking into the London Broncos first team in 2003.

Mbu was nine when he arrived in England from Kinshasa as an asylum seeker, having fled his homeland with his mother, two sisters and brother after his father, a teacher, was shot dead during the civil unrest that plagued the former Belgian colony for more than a decade. The country is more stable these days and had its first democratic elections in 2006, but for Mbu it now seems like another world. "They play with guns like they play with matches over there," is his rather blunt and depressing statement.

The subject of his father, Zizi, is an emotional one. Mbu does not mind talking about him, it is just that he remembers little of what happened, both at the time and the immediate aftermath. He recalls coming to England with his mother, Dorcas, two elder sisters, Carene and Lydei, and younger brother, Rsti. He recalls being housed in temporary accommodation near Heathrow Airport before moving permanently to north London. But what evokes most memories from that time was his attempts to learn English. "Looking back, it was funny," said Mbu, who shares a flat in Wimbledon with team-mate Tyrone Smith. "I spoke two different languages - French and Lingala - and had another one to learn. Sometimes I would get a word wrong but I was convinced I was right until someone could show me otherwise. For a long time, I used to think 'my name is' was pronounced and spelt 'mayonnaise'."

Flying the flag for London

Young guns – four Londoners making an impact on the game.
Clockwise from top left: Tony Clubb, Michael Worrincy,
Louie McCarthy-Scarsbrook and Joe Mbu. (Photos: Philip Gordos)

Mbu is a softly spoken but confident individual. He is not physically imposing, but you can sense the power in his compact frame. He is a good build for a rugby league player, though the game was not his first sporting love. "I didn't want to have anything to do with it," said Mbu. "I thought rugby league was a funny sport, all those guys touching each other. It wasn't for me. I was playing a lot of football and basketball anyway. I was good enough as a kid to play football at a good standard and I was also invited to train with the London Leopards, a top basketball team." Whether it was football or basketball, Mbu says he relished physical confrontation. "I played centre-half in football and the strikers were scared of me," he said. "I used to intimidate them because they knew if I didn't get the ball then I would at least get them. I wasn't worried about getting bumps and bruises."

One of Mbu's cousins thought he would be perfect for rugby league and urged him to attend a training session with the London Skolars, who were based near his home. "I didn't go, but after two weeks my cousin told me that they gave him food after training," recalled Mbu. "I'm a big lover of food, so I went along for the nosh. The first training session, I loved it. I loved the contact. It is weird how things work out but it was my destiny to play rugby league."

Mbu took to the game like a duck to water. In fact, he was so good, one of the giants of the rugby league game came knocking on his door. "Wigan were very interested, but I chose to stay in London," he said. "I needed to be near my family and friends."

Family is hugely important to Mbu and he has nothing but respect and love for his mother. "I really look up to her, she is my hero," he said. "She is compassionate, but she also knew she had to discipline me when I was growing up. That is not an easy thing to do. It is hard for single mothers to give both discipline and love, but she was able to balance all of that. I grew up a lot quicker because I saw how hard things were for her and I never bothered her with small stuff. I was just grateful for anything she gave me. I appreciate everything she does for us."

Faith plays a big part in Mbu's life, too. A Christian, he goes to church every Sunday when he is not playing rugby. He is involved with the youth services and occasionally sings gospel, though he admits he is not the world's best singer. "Some people have raw talent, but they are not sure of themselves. Even though I don't have a great voice, I still give it my best. I hope they see that and get encouragement from seeing me do it. I'm a bit crazy like that. I'm not afraid to try something different, to throw myself in at the deep end."

Mbu has been hailed as a role model for the younger players coming through at Harlequins RL. "He is like a father figure to them even though he is only 22," said Phil Jones, the club's player performance manager. "He kicks them up the backside if he doesn't think they are working hard enough, but they respect him. They see what he has achieved and start to believe that maybe they can do what he does, too."

Jones is a key figure. Born in Warrington, he joined the club as a development officer in 1998 and has been an integral part of the drive to make rugby league popular in the schools and colleges of London. In his words he is responsible for "creating a pathway to the first team" for the youngsters at the club. So when he sees the likes of Worrincy and McCarthy-Scarsbrook breaking through, he takes a great deal of satisfaction and delight in their elevation to the first team. "It must be like one of your kids graduating, I imagine," he said. "I'm like a proud parent at times."

Every Super League club has a player performance manager, a position part-funded by the Rugby Football League. But it is fair to say the role Jones occupies is pretty unique. Compared to places such as Wigan, Hull and Widnes, the game of rugby league is still developing in London, which poses its own set of problems and challenges. However, the rate at which the sport is growing in the capital gives Jones and the rest of the community team at Harlequins RL a great deal of optimism for the future. Like the untapped oil and gas fields in the old Soviet Union, Quins have a rich source of raw material on their doorstep. It is just a matter of accessing and refining it.

"We started off by deliberately targeting those schools where there wasn't much provision for sport," said Jones. "We knew we were always going to be competing against football, but we felt we had a chance against other sports. Kids weren't even aware there were two codes of rugby to start with, but rugby league was simple for them to understand and they were able to crack the basics within four weeks."

The inroads Jones and his team have made is staggering. According to the sport's governing body in this country, London and the South East is the fastest growing rugby league area in the United Kingdom. In fact, Greater London had 101 teams playing the game at the start of 2006. Only Leeds, Wakefield, Hull and Wigan had more. What is really encouraging, though, is the number of schools now playing the game. Nearly 300 of the region's primary and secondary institutions play rugby league. "There's a big ethnic mix," said Jones. "We've got Nigerians, Indians, West Indians and kids from places like Iraq. I'm really pleased it's like that. There's also a real mix of backgrounds. We have kids from The London Oratory School, where Prime Minister Tony Blair has sent some of his children, alongside kids from

Peckham. It's interesting to see how they interact with each other." But there are significant hurdles to overcome, like the length of time kids have to spend travelling. "People in the north forget or don't know that some of our players have to travel almost two hours before they even get on the team bus for an away game," he said. "It's not like St Helens, when a 20-minute journey is seen as a long way."

Jones was originally based in south-east London, when the club played at The Valley, but now the focus has shifted back towards west and south-west London following the move to Brentford and subsequent link-up with NEC Harlequins. He was sad to leave behind the work the club did in the Charlton and Greenwich regions, but he still gets players making the trip across London to play at the academy's new home at Imber Court. He also says there is a significant difference in the type of kids they are working with now. According to Jones, the players in south and south-east London are "bigger, stronger and have got a lot of dog in them". Those in the west and south-west are "more skilful with the ball".

The move to the Stoop has inevitably helped the spread of rugby league in and around London. "I feel like a lot of doors have been opened - and it's down to the name," said Jones. "I thought we might have some explaining to do now that we were called Harlequins rather than the London Broncos, but we haven't had to. The publicity has obviously worked and the reaction we've had has been positive. When we were the Broncos, one in every five people we made contact with seemed to ask us if we were an American Football team. Some players still think they can use us as vehicle to get into rugby union, but I've got great belief in our product and the opportunities we can offer. In rugby union, there isn't an under-18s competition, but there is in rugby league. That means we play the likes of Leeds and Bradford every week. It's a big draw."

Inevitably, Harlequins RL have had to tread a little carefully. Their work in such areas as Richmond, Kingston and Hounslow means they can end up competing for the same players that their union partners are interested in. But so far there has not been any fall-out. Jones realises that union clubs may have the pick of the talent, but he says he is confident of unearthing a few hidden gems. His growing list of local contacts, in particular the burgeoning relationship with St Mary's College in Twickenham, has been a big help in that regard. "We are developing a great relationship with St Mary's," said Jones, who is now head coach of the college's first team. "They cannot get enough of us at the moment. They had 10 to 12 players training when they first started. Now they've got two teams and a pool of around 40, which means some players don't even get a game."

Dan Steel and Dave Melling are just two members of the Harlequins RL community team responsible for spreading the gospel of rugby league in London. These are the guys at the coal face, the ones attempting to get their proverbial foot in the door. "People in the capital are a lot more enthusiastic and knowledgeable about rugby league than I thought," said Steel, who hails from Halifax and is a former full-back with Siddal ARLFC. "I had the impression that no one knows much or cares about the game in London, but that's not the case at all. I had the chance of a job at Leeds before I came here, but it's like preaching to the converted up there. Down here, it's exciting to be breaking new ground. I've always been a believer in having a top rugby league side in the capital, so I feel like I am helping spread the gospel." It is a sentiment echoed by Melling, who is keen to get the game into as many schools as possible. He feels the partnership with Harlequins has only helped in that respect. "The Harlequins name is an obvious plus point," said the Wiganer, who played amateur rugby league with Leyland Warriors. "It gets us in the door, then it is up to us to do our stuff."

Success on the pitch will no doubt facilitate the work of Harlequins RL and the Rugby Football League in London. Unfortunately for Quins, any hopes they had in 2006 of a second appearance in a Challenge Cup Final were dashed on Sunday 4 June. In a game screened live by the BBC, the Leeds Rhinos won their quarter-final clash 36-18 at Headingley. The result was a big let-down for Quins fans, many of whom had taken advantage of the free transport being laid on by the club to make the journey up the M1 to Yorkshire. Having beaten Harlequins RL twice already in 2006 - three times if you include the pre-season friendly - Leeds were odds-on favourites to make the semi-finals. But a spluttering first-half performance from the home side, during which Quins had several opportunities to score, gave the visitors cause for optimism. Leeds led 12-0 at the break but were soon ahead by only two points thanks to Dorn's try following a McLinden break and an opportunist score from Worrincy after good work by Nick Bradley-Qalilawa, who exploited some lazy Leeds defending.

But just when the Quins supporters had started dreaming of a shock win and a place in the last four, Ali Lauitiiti exploded off the Rhinos bench to wreck their hopes for another season. The giant New Zealand international, with better ball skills than the Harlem Globetrotters, ripped the heart out of the visitors as Leeds, coached on the day by Brian McDermott after Tony Smith was taken to hospital with gastroenteritis, scored four tries in just nine second-half minutes. It was a ruthless display and left Quins coach Tony Rea lamenting what might have been. "We were well and truly in the game midway through the second half," he said. "With a bit more authority we could have taken control." Sadly for Harlequins RL, it was another case of what might have been but they would hear a lot more about McDermott before the end of the season.

Feeling the heat in France

Nick Bradley-Qalilawa in action against Catalans Dragons.
(Photo: David Williams)

Tyrone Smith fights his way through the Catalans defence.
(Photo: David Williams)

Matchday at The Twickenham Stoop

Queuing for a coffee at the first home match against Castleford – the facilities at the Stoop were much better than at Griffin Park.

Left: the beer sellers stop for a break. Above: Ball boys get ready for action.

The Harlequin Hearts strut their stuff before the Salford match.
(All photos: Peter Lush)

8. Bright lights, big city

"I got on the tube and there were people everywhere, pushing you out of the way. But you get used to it, London is a way of life."
Paul Sykes, Harlequins RL player

Their Challenge Cup dreams over for another year, Harlequins RL turned their attentions to Super League. With just 11 points from 15 games, it seemed their main objective was avoiding relegation, an unimaginable scenario at the start of the season given all the hopes and expectations generated by the move to the Stoop. Yet their plight was not as dire as results suggested. With Wigan rooted to the foot of the table, having won just two league games all season, Quins were seven points clear of bottom place. Amazingly, they were also just five points off the sixth and final play-off spot occupied by Salford. There was still plenty to play for, starting with the visit of fifth-placed Warrington Wolves.

The Wolves were a hard side to judge in 2006. Before the season began they were generally regarded as an automatic choice for the play-offs. They had a highly-respected coach in Paul Cullen and a string of top-class players in Lee Briers, Martin Gleeson, Henry Fa'afili and Paul Rauhihi. They were regarded as a club on the move, poised to challenge the big five of St Helens, Bradford, Leeds, Wigan and Hull. Such was their blossoming status that they appeared to be winning the race to sign Adrian Morley. The Great Britain forward was coming to the end of his contract with the Sydney Roosters and was coveted by virtually every club in Super League. But the Wolves looked to be favourites to bag a player who boasted one of the most feared and respected reputations in the world game.

Yet for all their star talent and promise, Warrington had failed to set Super League alight in 2006. They had beaten Leeds and Bradford only to suffer a surprise home defeat against French newcomers Catalans Dragons. They had also been beaten twice by Salford at the Halliwell Jones Stadium. It was a real mixed bag of results and had left them trailing the big guns they were desperately trying to emulate. But then came arguably the biggest setback of the lot, a shock Challenge Cup reverse at the hands of Hull Kingston Rovers. The trip to Craven Park was never going to be a walk in the park, but few expected the unbeaten National League 1 leaders to emerge triumphant. What followed was a match of stunning intensity, the home side defying the odds to seal their place in the semi-finals. Wolves led early on thanks to two tries but trailed 24-22 at half-time as the Robins bounced back in style. The home side's advantage grew until Warrington gave themselves a glimmer of hope with two late scores. But it proved too little too late for the visitors.

Warrington needed a win over Harlequins RL on 10 June to boost their flagging spirits. But Quins were just as desperate for victory. It showed, too. Three late tries from the Wolves made the score close, but Quins had ended the game as a contest by taking a 26-6 lead midway through the second half. Michael Worrincy set the ball rolling by diving over after 11 minutes before Rob Purdham crossed for a 12-0 lead at the break. Pat Weisner, Henry Paul and Solomon Haumono added further tries after the interval before Wolves staged their late, but ultimately fruitless, comeback in the last five minutes.

What made the home side's 30-28 win all the more satisfying was that they had beaten Warrington without skipper Mark McLinden, Danny Williams, Lee Hopkins, Thomas Leuluai and Matt Gafa, who were all sidelined by injury. Hopkins, an ever-present since joining the club at the start of 2005, had been in line for his 50th successive appearance but had broken a hand in the Cup defeat by Leeds the previous week. "The chase is on for a play-off spot," said a delighted Tony Rea, whose side were now up to seventh in the table.

Standing in the way of a third straight league win for Harlequins RL and even more upward momentum were Hull FC. A victory at the Kingston Communications Stadium in March gave the Quins players cause for optimism ahead of another trip north. But the Hull side they faced on Friday 16 June bore little resemblance to the one they had beaten 10-6 earlier in the season. The players may have been the same, but the man in charge now was Australian Peter Sharp, who had succeeded John Kear in April. Sharp, a former assistant coach with Parramatta Eels, had transformed Hull's fortunes, giving them the belief that they could really challenge the best Super League had to offer. They lay third in the table, just two points behind Leeds, and had just inflicted a rare defeat on leaders St Helens. The 27-26 victory, achieved thanks to Paul Cooke's dramatic drop-goal in the dying seconds, was Hull's first win at Knowsley Road for 18 years and their eighth league success on the trot.

Luke Dorn's early try must have raised hopes of another surprise win at the KC Stadium for Quins, but it proved to be a false dawn. Hull recovered to lead at half-time before closing out a 30-16 victory. It was their ninth in a row, equalling a club record, but Sharp had other things on his mind rather than a place in the history books when he faced the media after the match. He praised his players but wasted little time in taking a few pot-shots at the tactics of the visiting team. "If they were a cricket side, they would get fined for a slow over rate," said the disgruntled Australian, who clearly felt Quins had done all they could within the laws of the game to deny Hull quick ball. "It was a pretty dour old game but I never felt as though they put us under any pressure," he added. "I thought we had their measure." The comments riled the normally unflappable Tony Rea, who responded in kind. After lambasting Sharp's comments as "boring and pathetic", he urged his countryman to worry about his own side rather than the opposition's.

The after-match verbals made good copy for the newspapers, but they were of little consequence to Jon Wells. Disappointed as he was with the defeat at Hull, his overriding emotion was one of delight and relief at having made his first competitive appearance of 2006. After spending the first half of the season stuck on the sidelines nursing a string of unfortunate injuries, he had made an unexpected comeback at the KC Stadium. "I thought I would get a couple of games with the under-21s first but then I was suddenly on the bench," explained Wells. "Then, when Matt Gafa pulled out, I found I was starting on the left wing. My first tackle was a real shock to me. I'd not done any contact work for eight months because of my broken nose, then my jaw and then my foot. But once I got the first hit out of the way, I was okay. It was tough lasting the entire 80 minutes, though."

Wells paid tribute to team-mate Tyrone Smith for helping him out during the game, but most of his praise was reserved for Harlequins RL conditioner Thibault Giroud. "Thibault has kept me in as good a shape as he could while I was out injured," said Wells. "He advised me a lot about my diet because I couldn't train properly and needed to watch the calories."

Wells admitted it had been hard being out of action for so long. "You don't realise just how much you miss everything until you have to spend a long time on the sidelines," he said. "It has shown me how much I love the game and how privileged I am to do what I do for a living. Being able to train with the guys without having to go off and see the physio or the specialist and have an X-ray or scan has been a breath of fresh air, too. But now I've got the opportunity to really contribute. It's a really good feeling to know that if we get some success this season I will have played my part."

The defeat at Hull was a setback for Quins but results elsewhere had been kind. Castleford, Wigan and Wakefield had won, but Warrington, Salford and Huddersfield had all lost, ensuring Quins remained just five points off the play-offs. "It keeps us within touching distance of the top six," added Wells. "If we can pick up four points from our next two games, we will really be in the shake-up." Those two games were against Catalans Dragons and Wigan, who had just recorded only their third league win of the season, an unconvincing 24-18 victory over the Dragons at the JJB Stadium. The Warriors were still bottom of the table with a measly six points, but they had at least convinced the talismanic Kris Radlinski to end his brief retirement in an effort to preserve their top-flight status. Still, the future looked bleak for Wigan, and Wells was looking forward to making it bleaker. "I have some sympathy for Wigan," he said. "But it would be nice to be the team that hammers another nail in their coffin." First, though, there was the matter of a trip to the south of France.

Catalans Dragons had exceeded many people's expectations in their first season in Super League. They had upset Wigan on the opening weekend, shocked Warrington at the Halliwell Jones Stadium and had beaten Castleford home and away by the time Harlequins RL made the journey to Stade Aime Giral on 24 June. The influence of Stacey Jones had been key, but so had the form of the lesser-known players, like Australian winger Justin Murphy, New Zealand forward Alex Chan and home favourites Jamal Fakir and Julien Rinaldi. Michael Dobson, recruited temporarily to fill the gap left by Jones when the New Zealand stand-off was sidelined with a broken arm early in the season, had also made his mark, so much so that he had been snapped up by Wigan when Jones had returned to full fitness. Still, Quins travelled to Perpignan in good heart. When they opened up a 12-0 lead after just 11 minutes, a seventh league win of the season looked on the cards. But then everything went wrong. The Dragons recovered to lead 20-12 at half-time and took complete control when Mark McLinden and Danny Williams were sin-binned in rapid succession after the break. Murphy finished with two tries while Jones kicked 14 points in a 38-18 victory for the home side. It was a major setback for Quins.

Karl Temata scored his first try of the season in the loss to Catalans. It was scant consolation for the former New Zealand Warriors forward, who was in his first full season with the club. A favourite with Quins fans, he had spent several weeks on the sidelines with a torn pectoral muscle that was to plague him for the entire campaign. A powerful runner, the dreadlocked Kiwi loved nothing more than bashing opposing defenders out of his way on one of his trademark bullocking runs down the middle of the park. It was his speed that made him such a dangerous player. But then he had begun life in the backs. Daniel Anderson, his coach at the Warriors, is the man who decided Temata's future lay in the second-row. "I was a bit surprised when he told me what he was doing, but I had no choice really," said Temata. "Second-row is not such a big step from centre and I probably prefer playing there anyway."

Born in Whangarei, New Zealand's northernmost city, Temata was a latecomer to professional rugby league. He had played both union and league as a youngster but taken neither too seriously. When he enrolled at the University of Otago in Dunedin to study physical education and geography, rugby of either code went on the backburner completely. "I wasn't serious enough to give it a chance," he said. "I was more into being a student and mucking around. Dad was constantly in my ear. He wanted me to start playing league again because he thought I could make a go of it. He was constantly on about the World Cup in 2000 because I was eligible to play for the Cook Islands through my grandfather."

His father's badgering and the appeal of playing on the international stage eventually proved too much for Temata. At the end of 1999, he dropped out of university, moved to Auckland and started playing for Hibiscus Coast Raiders while working during the day as a scaffolder. "I started at 6.45am and was finished by 3pm, so that gave me time to train," he said. "It was difficult to balance work and training, but I felt it was worth the effort." Hibiscus were coached by Brian McClennan, who went on to take charge of the New Zealand national side. "He was a very good coach and I had a few really happy years there," said Temata. "That's when I started to take the game seriously."

Temata achieved his goal of playing in the 2000 World Cup. The Cook Islands, 15 tiny islands spread over 850,000 square miles in the middle of the South Pacific Ocean, were fielding a side in the competition for the first time. Their only player of note was captain Kevin Iro, the former Wigan, Leeds and St Helens centre who had made 31 Test appearances for New Zealand. Yet, they had previously shown some form, claiming the scalps of the USA, Russia, Scotland and finally Ireland to win the 1995 Emerging Nations tournament. The World Cup was clearly a step up, but it was all part of the building process. For Temata, the competition was a chance to pit himself against some of the best players around and discover how he measured up. He started well, scoring his side's first try of the competition against Wales. The score helped tie the match at 6-6 before the Welsh, with Lee Briers and Iestyn Harris in their side, went on to record a 36-6 victory in Wrexham. The Cook Islands were crushed 84-10 by New Zealand in their next game in Reading before finishing their group campaign with a 22-22 draw against fellow minnows Lebanon at the Millennium Stadium in Cardiff. In the first ever rugby league international to be played under a closed roof, Temata's side led

22-10 with just five minutes left only to squander the chance of a well-deserved win. Canterbury Bulldogs winger Hazem El-Mazri rescued a point for Lebanon, scoring a try and then kicking a last-minute conversion from the touchline. It was a disappointing finish for the Cook Islands, but Temata had enjoyed his brief spell in the spotlight. "The tournament was my first experience of playing against really good teams and I thought I was up to it," said Temata. "It was a good gauge and gave me more motivation to keep going."

Temata continued to play for Hibiscus, helping them win the Bartercard Cup, the New Zealand national championship, in 2001, but he soon caught the eye of the New Zealand Warriors. He began training with the NRL club twice a week after work. He was joined in the so-called "night squad" by other up-and-coming players looking to force their way into the big time, the most notable of which was Iafeta Palea'aesina, now at Wigan and still a close pal of Temata's. Finally, at the end of the 2002 season and with the Warriors already crowned Minor Premiers, Temata was given his first-team debut in a home game against Wests Tigers. "I suffered from nerves in that game and knocked on with my first touch," recalled Temata, who started the match on the interchange bench with Palea'aesina. "I couldn't believe it. It was not the best way to start, but I was okay after that." It was a winning debut for Temata. The Warriors, with the likes of Henry Fa'afili, Francis Meli, Motu Tony, Logan Swann and Mark Tookey in the side, beat Wests 26-12 in front of more than 16,000 fans at the Ericsson Stadium. Temata did not play again that season, but the Warriors went on to reach the Grand Final, losing 30-8 to the Sydney Roosters.

Temata became a fully paid-up professional with the Warriors the following year and enjoyed plenty of game time. He quickly flourished under Anderson's guidance. "He taught me a lot," said Temata. "Having started quite late in the game, I had to catch up on my skills. Anderson was big on the basics and was very keen on getting the little things right." Anderson steered the Warriors into the play-offs again the following season before losing out to eventual winners Penrith Panthers. But when things went awry in 2004, he decided to quit midway through the season. Temata remained a first-team regular under new boss Tony Kemp but decided he, too, wanted a change at the end of 2005. Temata had always fancied trying his luck in Super League, but with Tookey and Thomas Leuluai, another former Warriors team-mate, already in London, the prospect of a move to the English capital appealed to him more than any other. Temata was initially going to join the Broncos at the start of the 2006 season, but, with the Warriors already done and dusted for the season after missing out on the play-offs, he was offered the chance to come across sooner. "I jumped at the opportunity," said Temata, who made three appearances for the Broncos at the end of 2005, scoring a try in the 68-10 win over Widnes that secured the team a place in the play-offs.

London has become a magnet for Australians and Kiwis. Keen to take in all the city has to offer, they also use it as a base from which to make trips into the rest of Europe. Some end up staying in the capital for a week or two, others end up staying for years. Like Steele Retchless. "London is one of the best cities in the world and I lived there for seven years," said the former Broncos forward. "My kids still remember stuff we did, like visiting the London Eye, and my wife says she would love to come back. It was sometimes really hard for her there, bringing up the kids when I was away a lot with the team, but she also must have loved it. You miss the little things more than anything else. We used to have a family day on Wednesday when we'd drive into Kingston and have lunch somewhere. That was fantastic."

For Retchless, who now works for a wine company back in his native Australia, one of the big plusses of life in a big city is being able to walk the streets incognito. "In London, you can go down the pub and have a couple of beers without anyone bothering you or recognising who you were, no problem," said the former second rower. "I loved talking to the fans after the game, but I also liked being anonymous. The odd Broncos fan would come up in the supermarket and that was great. I'd talk to them for five minutes. But after a game, you could go out and have a few beers as if you were just another Aussie backpacker." As if to emphasise the value of anonymity, Retchless recalled an incident during a Super League match against Widnes. It was during an on-the-road game in Wales, played there because Griffin Park was unavailable, and a whole load of Vikings fans had made the trek to watch their team. But when the Broncos opened up a 30-0 lead at half-time, the Widnes supporters started having a go at their own players. The level of performance obviously rankled but that was not their chief beef. According to Retchless, they were unhappy because several members of the Widnes team now floundering about in front of their very eyes had been spotted having "a few beers" during the week. It was, in short, like waving a red rag in front of a bull. "The Widnes fans were yelling at their team to get off the booze," said Retchless. "It was not a nice sight."

Tulsen Tollett also loved being just a face in the London crowd. "For me, it was nice to be able to go out without people watching your every step," said the former Great Britain international, who played alongside Retchless for the Broncos. It is a sentiment echoed by most players who have played for the club. However, not everyone was happy being ignored. According to Tollett, former Australian Test prop Mark Carroll needed his ego massaging once in a while. "He needed the attention," said Tollett. "If he was recognised by anyone, even if it was backpacker on the tube, he would ditch his team-mates and go off to talk to them." A much-hyped signing for the 1998 season, Carroll went home after just a year with the Broncos. He re-signed for South Sydney and became a personal bodyguard for Oscar-winning actor Russell Crowe, ensuring he was never far from the limelight.

Tollett was 22 years old when he joined the Broncos in 1996. A Great Britain tourist, representing the Lions on the 1996 tour to Papua New Guinea and New Zealand, he had been born in Hastings on the south coast of England before emigrating to Australia with his parents. He has nothing but fond memories of his time with the Broncos, helping them to record a famous win over Canberra Raiders in the 1997 World Club Championship series and reach the Challenge Cup final in 1999. In fact, he liked London so much he chose to remain when a persistent shoulder injury eventually forced him into premature retirement at the end of 2001.

He admits London has its drawbacks, like traffic congestion, but says it has plenty to offer, too. "If you are prepared to do things, like take in the culture, it's a great place to be," he said. "There's more to life than just playing rugby after all. It's not just about training and playing and then going home. It's about getting out and doing things." Without sounding like a spokesman for London Mayor Ken Livingstone, the city's appeal is huge. But then spending a few days taking in the sights is a totally different experience to living and working there.

One thing London does not have is a beach. If it did, it would just about be the perfect place on earth for Tony Rea. "I surfed from when I was six or seven, so I miss that massively," said the Quins coach. "When I am back in Australia, I make sure I take my board out a couple of times." Rea has spent a decade in the capital, but he says he only really began to discover just what the city had to offer once he had hung up his boots. "When you are playing you don't really live London," he said. "It has so many attractions, such a pulse, but when you're playing you cannot really enjoy it. In that respect it is not particularly different to anywhere else. But once you stop playing you can really get out and enjoy the culture and people of London. It is not a particularly healthy lifestyle here – there is a lot of rushing about and a lot of drinking going on - but it is a really enjoyable place to be. I'm a restaurants man myself, that is my big thing. I usually spend my time ducking off for a meal, having a chat with a glass of wine or a beer."

Rea and his family can envisage making a permanent home for themselves in London. Had you put such a proposition to countryman Mark McLinden within a few months of his arrival in the capital, he would have thought you were crazy. Why anyone would want to swap what Australia had to offer – the weather, the outdoor lifestyle and such like – for life in a crowded, polluted city like London was beyond him. Now, however, he is starting to come around to Rea's way of thinking and can see himself spending a long time here. "I'm starting to feel really at home here," said the former Canberra Raiders player. "I didn't get the English humour at first, but I think I've cracked it now."

McLinden lived with Danny Williams when the two Australians first arrived in London at the end of 2004. They spent a lot of their spare time seeing the sights of the capital but thought nothing of jumping on an aeroplane and heading for mainland Europe. Prague, Alicante, Biarritz, San Sebastian and Majorca are just a few of the places they visited. They also flew to Dusseldorf with three team-mates, Anthony Armour, Mark O'Halloran and Nick Bradley-Qalilawa. It was a spur of the moment thing, a question of surfing the internet with no particular destination in mind. It was all about cheap flights and cheap hotels for the self-styled Dusseldorf Five. "That's what I love about London," said Williams. "It's the doorstep to Europe. The city itself offers so much variety, so much to see and do. It's not everyone's cup of tea, but I've got no regrets about coming here at all."

There are lots of reasons why London has become a haven for players from the southern hemisphere. Certainly when Super League began in 1996, the only way of ensuring the team was competitive was by filling it with Australians, Kiwis and Pacific Islanders. There were one or two big signings from the north of England, like Martin Offiah and Shaun Edwards, but not too many more from the so-called rugby league heartlands were keen on moving to the capital. For some, the hustle and bustle of London just did not appeal. Neither did its prices, from the cost of a pint of lager to the cost of a family home. Others were simply reluctant to uproot their families. But there is a genuine hope that the tide is turning, that London is becoming more attractive to players from the north of the country. "I have been here for six years now and I've enjoyed living in London," said Paul Sykes, who swapped life in Bradford for life in the capital in 2001. "The rushing about was something I noticed when I first arrived. I got on the tube and there were people everywhere, pushing you out of the way. But you get used to it, London is a way of life."

Fellow Yorkshireman John Wells says he was very much used to village life before moving to London. "Coming down here was a real eye opener," he said. "But I like being busy with things to do, and there is plenty to do in London."

The number of local boys coming through the ranks, the likes of Michael Worrincy, Tony Clubb and Louie McCarthy-Scarsbrook, is also helping Harlequins RL move away from its perceived over-reliance on overseas players. With the number of quota spots down to four in 2007 and then three in 2008, falling in line with the rest of Super League, the club realises it has no choice but to change its outlook on recruitment. "It needs to get away from being a home-away-from-home for Aussies and Kiwis," said Luke Dorn. "The club needs to entice some quality English players here. They need a Stuart Fielden, a Sean Long or a Paul Sculthorpe." Fans of Harlequins RL can only dream.

9. A boy from Bundaberg

"Sometimes you have got to pull yourself up, push your head above the clouds and have a look around."
Tony Rea, Harlequins RL director and former coach

Tony Rea loves coffee. Some of the staff at Harlequins RL joke that he cannot function without his regular intake of caffeine. In the week between the crucial home games against Wigan and Castleford at the start of July, Rea was relaxing at the club's training ground at Roehampton Vale with a cup of his favourite beverage. The telephone rang, as it does often. Rea answered and began a conversation that effectively brought to an end his six-year tenure as head coach.

The previous Saturday Quins had come up against a Wigan team propping up the Super League table. For supporters of the proud Lancashire club, it was a sad state of affairs, but not nearly as sorry as it had been. Wigan had won just one of their first eight games and spent the early months of the season familiarising themselves with the lower reaches of the table.

Now, with Great Britain coach Brian Noble pulling the strings from the stands, and £450,000 summer signing Stuart Fielden leading from the front on the pitch, Wigan's position no longer looked hopeless. By the time they came to The Twickenham Stoop on Saturday 1 July, they were just four points adrift of safety thanks in part to victories over Catalans and Warrington, their first back-to-back successes in Super League XI. Quins, in contrast, had lost twice since their narrow defeat of Warrington and their fans, who were used to adversity, were starting to feel the cold hand of desperation enveloping them once again.

"The match could be a turning point. If Quins lose, the pressure is really on. Win and the pressure is off," wrote one supporter on an internet message board. Another added: "The time has come for the Quins to stand up and be counted. "Certain players are not performing to their capabilities (they know who they are)."

The first half was as tough and uncompromising as one would expect in a game of such obvious importance. Quins scored tries through Solomon Haumono and Pat Weisner, though both unquestionably had a hint of fortune about them. Haumono did not look like he had grounded the ball. Weisner appeared to fall short of the line before the ball was ripped from his grasp. Karl Kirkpatrick referred both to the video referee, who twice came down on the side of the Quins. There was no doubt about the quality of the decisions in the mind of Fielden, who described them as a "joke". The tries ensured that Quins were level at the break, with Chris Ashton and Brett Dallas crossing for the visitors.

A Michael Dobson penalty early in the second half put Wigan back in front only for Quins to respond with a try from Joe Mbu and a third conversion from Henry Paul. The home side led 18-14, but the match - and two crucial Super League points - hung in the balance until tries from Mark Calderwood and Ashton, his second of the day, gave Wigan a decisive eight-point advantage. Mark McLinden crossed for Quins with six minutes remaining, Paul adding the extra points, but it was not enough to stop the home side from slumping to a third straight defeat.

Harlequins RL supporters took the 26-24 defeat hard. "I've got to say that I am at my lowest ebb ever since starting to follow the club 10 years ago," wrote one. "I have never seen a side of ours play with less commitment."

Rea admitted his side's error count had proved costly. "We were close but not close enough and it is a huge disappointment," he lamented. "We need to get a little run together, to build some momentum, but we have not really had one of those all season." The loss, their 12th from 19 games, left Quins down in ninth spot, just three points above Wigan and one ahead of Wakefield and Catalans. Next up was a home game against Castleford, who were up to seventh thanks to a 52-26 demolition of Warrington. Rea knew it was a pivotal game. A fourth straight defeat would leave the club with all sorts of problems. But he was used to pressure.

Rea was born on 25 July 1966 to parents who were teachers in the bush town of Bundaberg, four hours north of Brisbane in the Australian state of Queensland. His dad played league, either as a full-back or stand-off, while his brother Michael was a talented half-back who might have made a career out of the game.

However, he preferred to stay in Bundaberg and lives there to this day. Tony, in contrast, ended up 12,000 miles away in London. Talk to Rea about his childhood and it is clear it was a happy and contented time. He is passionate for the outdoor life, like most Aussies, and loved surfing. It is one of the things he misses most about his homeland. When he was not out on the water, Rea spent most of his spare time playing or watching rugby league. Bundaberg, a town famous the world over for its rum, was a rugby league hotbed. It had a main oval surrounded by four smaller ones, all of which were used to play the game. The action usually took place on the weekend, starting at 9am and lasting the whole day.

The kids would be up first, followed by the older teams. Rea, who joined the local team, the Bundaberg Brothers, as a five-year-old, would stay all day. "I would get some lunch money and stick around after my game was over, often doing a bit as a ball boy," he recalled. Rea played in a variety of positions, not unusual for a youngster learning his rugby in the bush, but by the age of 12 his career as a hooker had begun. "It was in the days when scrums were contested," said Rea. "The old bloke, our coach, said that I was to play hooker for a game and to try to win some scrums. I won some but when I came off the field my shoulders were really sore from all the pushing and I just thought to myself 'never again'. The old bugger walked over and said 'right, you're playing there for the rest of the season'." That 'old bugger' Rea affectionately refers to is Noel Cavanagh, the former Australian international who was to become a key figure in Rea's life.

Rea played hard and enjoyed his rugby. If you ask him how good he was, expect an understated answer. But by the time he was 16, he had secured a three-year scholarship with the Brisbane Brothers. It was his display in a Queensland schoolboys carnival that sealed his move. Bundaberg were not faring particularly well in the tournament - such a small town was not expected to – so Rea's dad pulled him to one side and gave him some advice that would make all the difference. "I'll never forget what he told me," said Rea. "He said I could carry on as I was going – he said I was playing okay - or I could make a decision. He said I should touch the ball three times in every set and try to dominate the game. He told me to forget about winning and losing, that I had to look after myself. I really ripped into the carnival and won the scholarship. From then on, I really took the game seriously."

Having hardly ever been out of Bundaberg, moving to Brisbane was a big step for Rea. "It was a dream, though it was scary at first," he said. "But after starting in January, I got through to Easter and never looked back." As part of his scholarship Rea acquired coaching badges, referees badges, medical certificates and the like. In addition to his rugby development, the scholarship gave Rea the opportunity to study maths at North Brisbane University, 15 hours a week for three years.

Why study maths? "I like maths," is his immediate response. Rea has no time for what he terms "short cutters", never has, and as a scholarship student he worked hard to maximise the talent he had. "I trained really hard, probably harder than anyone, but then I always did," he said.

"I had my disappointments. There were times when I missed my spots and did not get picked, but I just kept working." He enjoyed some success with the Brisbane Brothers club, winning Queensland's Grand Final at a packed Laing Park in 1987. "There was a real buzz running out and I remember parts of that game really well," he added.

Then came another bold move. In 1988, the Brisbane Broncos decided to join the New South Wales Rugby League Championship, the forerunner to the National Rugby League. "It changed the landscape in Brisbane totally, certainly for my team, the Brothers," said Rea. "We had a meeting with our coach, who said it would never be the same in Brisbane again." Rea, now 21, had to make a decision. Should he stay put or try to further his career? He decided to join the North Sydney Bears, a rival of the Brisbane Broncos in the NSWRL. He also accepted his first major teaching job, in mathematics naturally, at St Aloysius' College in Kirribilli. "It was situated right under Sydney Harbour Bridge looking out to the Opera House," said Rea. "It was surreal at times, a boy from Bundaberg looking out of the classroom window at that sight."

Rea has fond memories of his time in the classroom. "Kids are funny buggers and absolutely brutal, even with their teachers," he said. "If I did well in a game I would get to school on a Monday and there would be eight or nine kids at the gate telling me what a great game I'd had. But if Norths had lost, there would be about 48 of them there, all rubbing it in."

In 1991, Norths went full-time but Rea's short-lived teaching career had already ended the year before when he took a job with a sports marketing firm. For a couple of years, he lived close to the beach in Manly and was able to indulge his passion for surfing. But his focus continued to be rugby. Rea spent seven seasons with Norths and experienced a great deal of success. "It was a really good time," he said. "It was a club that was struggling when I got there but by the time I left it was near the top, a bit like the Brisbane Brothers." By the end of the 1994 season, Rea was growing increasingly frustrated. He was unhappy with some of the coaching staff at the club and said as much to Denis Handlin, a friend of his and the boss of Sony Music in Australia. Handlin had lunch with a key mover at the Brisbane Broncos shortly afterwards and was told that the club were looking for someone to head up the rugby league franchise they had just invested in over in England, the London Crusaders. Rea, back in Bundaberg following the death of his grandmother, suddenly got a telephone call that was to change his life.

"When I got in after surfing, my dad told me that Brisbane Broncos had been on the phone. I didn't have any idea what he was talking about." He soon did. Rea held talks with the Broncos and decided to accept their offer of a job in London.

Rea arrived in the English capital in December 1994 and spent Christmas morning eating a breakfast of steak and eggs at team-mate Kevin Langer's house. Rea was prepared for his new lifestyle but still could not help but feel twinges of doubt in those first few months. He had lived in a top-floor apartment by the beach in Sydney. Now he was bedding down on the living room floor of Steve Rosolen's one-bedroom flat. Rea knew Rosolen well – they had been at kindergarten together – but it was still a major change. What's more, the weather was rubbish.

Rea had three seasons as a player with London before retiring at the age of 30 in 1996. He missed most of the short 1995 centenary season because of injury and felt that he was no longer able to do justice to himself. He had broken his leg three times, had undergone a shoulder reconstruction in 1995 and suffered from a bulging disc in his back for most of 1996. As far as he was concerned, the writing was on the wall. "There were a couple of times on the field where I knew what I wanted to do but the body let me down," said Rea. "I did not like that feeling, so I thought I would retire one season early rather than one late." Rea's final game was at St Helens. "I had made my decision and I was happy with it," he said. "I hung my boots on a hook after the game and that was it forever more."

A natural leader during his career, Rea had captained most of the teams he played for and wanted to pursue a career in coaching now that his playing days were over. He felt sure his best options lay back in Australia. But then he was offered the chance to become chief executive of the London Broncos. It was an unexpected turn of events. "It took some deciding, but once a decision is made I reckon it becomes easy," said Rea. He enjoyed his new job, finding that each day threw up different challenges and problems to solve. He approached it with his customary zeal. "It is about setting standards and ethics," he said. Not even the sticky issue of players' contracts could faze him, even if the players concerned were close friends.

"Peter Gill and Steve Rosolen were both great mates - I was godfather to their kids - but when it came to contracts, well, for me it was easy," said Rea. "The numbers had been worked out at boardroom level, but I could see them looking back at me across the desk as if to say 'Come on mate, give me a bit more, it is not your money we are talking about'. But I was still responsible for the club and the standards that had been set."

Rea missed playing, but only for a fleeting moment. "I was very busy, focused on what I had to do, but I remember driving to a ground for big games and thinking 'gee, I'd like to be playing tonight', but that was just two or three times," he said. Just when he was getting accustomed to life away from the changing room, he was thrown back in when head coach Dan Stains was dismissed in 1999. In its wisdom, the club decided Rea and Les Kiss should take charge of team affairs. "I thought Les should have done it on his own," said Rea, "but the board saw him as young rookie and wanted me to do some of the media work to take the pressure off him a little bit. I told them the idea sounded half-baked. I wanted an equal share." That is what happened, until the demands of being both coach and chief executive started to take its toll on Rea. "After coaching I'd go to the office at six in the evening to look after the chief executive stuff," he said. "I was working ridiculously long days and I thought something was going to break. There was too much going on." Rea eventually allowed Kiss to take sole responsibility for matters on the pitch, but he had enjoyed his time as coach. "I just did it," said Rea. "It was bizarre how easy it felt."

When Kiss returned home to Australia for family reasons at the end of the season, former Wigan boss John Monie was appointed as coach. Despite his pedigree, the Australian could not repeat the success he had enjoyed in Lancashire and left before the 2000 season was over. Rea was appointed caretaker coach and did such a good job he was offered the post full-time.

Or maybe the club saw him as the cheap option, wanting him to be coach and remain as chief executive. "I just said 'no way'," said Rea. "I threw it back to them, telling them it was either one or the other, not both. The board of directors had another meeting and I thought they would tell me to continue as chief executive. That's what I had in my head anyway. But they offered me the job of coach. I did not see that coming at all." Rea feels his work as an expert summariser for Sky had been instrumental in helping him get the job. He says the club had been impressed with his reading of the game, so much so that they wanted him to practice what he preached. Rea had a week off and went to David Hughes's villa in Lanzarote to consider his options. He decided that if the board had enough faith in him to offer him the role of coach, he would accept.

Now coach, he threw himself into his new job. He dropped his television work and severely restricted his social activities. "I remember thinking this was a big deal, I have to get my head around it," he said. It was not an auspicious start for Rea, though. "We lost the first four games, but I knew why we had lost and had no worries at all," he said. "We were too keen in a couple of games and that snowballed a bit, but I was confident we could put things right." So it proved. The Broncos won the next seven matches, eventually finishing sixth in the table.

Five years on, Rea again found himself in a situation that demanded a strong nerve and cool head. Wigan's revival had gathered pace while Harlequins RL seemed to be locked in a downward spiral. They needed a victory – and fast.

The visit of Castleford on Saturday 8 July was their next opportunity. It became evident on the morning of the game against the Tigers that there was more than just two points resting on the outcome. At the start of the week Rea had spoken with Ian Lenagan about the prospect of stepping down as coach after the match. It had not been an impulsive decision. In fact Rea and Lenagan had been discussing a coaching shake-up for several months. But now things were gathering pace. Brian McDermott, assistant coach at Leeds Rhinos, had been identified as Rea's successor and both Rea and Lenagan felt it was time to act. McDermott had already been down to London to hold separate meetings with both men, but the former Bradford Bulls and Great Britain prop was a wanted man. His burgeoning reputation had already secured him an offer to become head coach at another club, but only when the current season was over. Sensing they could jump to the head of the queue if they moved quickly, Rea and Lenagan decided to offer McDermott the chance to take over at Quins immediately.

"Brian's other offer would have meant him staying in the north, which had its attractions for him," recalled Rea, who suggested to Lenagan that they force his hand. "I thought that was a good strategy. What we did not want to do was get to a shoot-out at the end of the season."

On the Tuesday leading up to the game against Castleford, Rea telephoned Tony Smith, his close friend and opposite number at Leeds Rhinos, to discuss the prospect of offering McDermott the job immediately. He then put the proposition to McDermott, who wanted time to think the offer over. Rea initially thought McDermott would rebuff the chance to take over straight away but still hoped he would accept the job at the end of the season. But with the game against Cas looming fast, Rea could not afford to dwell too long on the future. His chief concern was preparing his team for Saturday's visit of the Tigers. Then, prior to Friday afternoon's training session, he took an unexpected call from Smith. The Leeds coach said his club were keen to avoid weeks of rumours and speculation and that if McDermott was going to join Quins then it had to happen now. "I called Ian Lenagan and David Hughes and we agreed to go for it," said Rea. Rea broke the news of McDermott's appointment to the players during training on Friday evening, adding that he would become director of football. The players were stunned. It was an emotional moment.

Rea had first floated the idea of stepping down as coach and assuming a more proactive role within the club during dinner with then chairman David Hughes, chief executive Nic Cartwright and director Keith Hogg some 18 months previously. The Australian had been head coach since the turn of the millennium and had begun to think of other ways he could help the club move forward. "There were a couple of thoughts in my mind," he said. "I felt we needed to take the next step, that we needed to progress from being just a team to becoming a club." As coach, he felt he had not had enough time to devote attention to the bigger picture. "All of our focus had been week to week," he said. "Sometimes you have got to pull yourself up, push your head above the clouds and have a look around a bit." However, 18 months ago the timing had not been quite right. At that stage, the club was once again experiencing several financial problems and its future was far from secure. "It was all about survival at that point," said Rea.

The arrival of Lenagan midway through 2005 suddenly moved the goalposts. Rea had several lengthy conversations with the new chairman and joint owner who agreed with a lot of his views for the future. Numerous discussions took place over the following months, Lenagan making it clear how important it was to get the structure of the club right in order for it to flourish. One of the first decisions they came to was to appoint a British coach. "The move to Harlequins had been massively positive but we needed to change the perception of the club," said Rea. "We have been regarded as a home for Australians and Kiwis, and we wanted to get away from that. We wanted a British coach, but they had to be good."

One of the first men the club targeted was Shaun Edwards, but the Wigan legend, who enjoyed two spells with the Broncos in the 1990s, made it clear he wanted to stay in rugby union. Undaunted, Harlequins RL continued their search but were in no hurry to make an appointment. "Ian kept indicating to me that I only had to initiate any changes when I was ready," said Rea. "But it was not about me, it was about when we found the right man or when the timing was right. If it was just about me, I'd have probably kept coaching forever."

Rea thought he had found the right man once he had interviewed McDermott. But there were still doubts about the timing. Both Rea and Lenagan initially had reservations about making the switch in July. "We didn't like that," said Rea. "We did not want to be seen to be a club that would change its coach midway through a season, but we had an opportunity to get the person we were after at that point, so we decided to do it."

Dawn over The Twickenham Stoop on 8 July promised a day bathed in sunshine for Tony Rea's last game in charge of Harlequins RL. But the weather was not the hot topic of conversation in the minds of the small coterie of journalists who regularly follow the fortunes of the club. It was not long before the telephones started buzzing with rumours of a shake-up at the club. Had Rea been sacked? Had he resigned? Who was taking over – and when? By mid-morning the picture was a little clearer. Yes, Rea would no longer be the coach after the game against Castleford, but there would be no official announcement until after the match.

All sorts of names were being bandied about as Rea's successor. Ian Millward and John Kear, who were both without a club after parting company with Wigan and Hull FC respectively earlier in the season, were on a lot of people's lips. So was Salford coach Karl Harrison. But the name that cropped up again and again was that of Leeds Rhinos assistant coach Brian McDermott. But if people at the club knew who was taking over, they certainly weren't saying.

Rea had spent the Friday evening focused on the game. He put to one side the dramatic events of the previous few hours but was moved by the texts and telephone calls that had flooded in from the players. In his match-day programme notes, written before he knew he was stepping down, Rea emphasised the need for unity. "We as a club always fight well when we fight together," he wrote. "Sometimes under pressure organisations pull apart and end up fighting amongst themselves." The sentiment held true whether Rea was on the move or not. Not that the Castleford supporters cared. They had seen their side win once already at the Stoop in 2006, overturning an early 14-0 deficit to triumph 34-20, and were in upbeat mood, clearly anticipating another win. Cries of "Yorkshire, Yorkshire" and "We hate cockneys" rang out from the North Stand.

From the opening kick to the final tackle, there was an intensity and focus to the home side's performance against Castleford that suggested the players were determined to make Rea's farewell a winning one. "The news had an impact I thought," mused Rea after the game. "It was the sort of lift you are looking for at that point in the season." Lee Hopkins made an early thunderous tackle on Michael Shenton that set the tone. It was Hopkins who scored the opening try, too, collecting a pass from Henry Paul before crossing. Mark McLinden put Quins further ahead before Willie Manu reduced the deficit.

Then came the first of two serious injuries. Tigers winger Waine Pryce went down in a heap near the halfway line in the middle of the pitch. It was immediately clear he was in a lot of trouble, both from the way he lay prone and the reaction from the players in the vicinity. Andy Henderson took one look at his team-mate's mangled left leg and reeled quickly away, covering his eyes and grimacing. The paramedics were soon on the field attending to the stricken Pryce, who was eventually stretchered off after 10 minutes of treatment. X-rays later revealed he had broken both the fibula and tibia, which meant the end of his season and a long lay-off. When the action began again, McLinden wasted little time in extending his side's advantage.

But it was not the only significant moment before the half-time hooter. As the teams trooped off to the dressing rooms, a Quins-clad figure lay motionless in the Castleford half of the field. It turned out to be Filomone Lolohea. The former South Sydney Rabbitohs prop, making a rare first-team appearance, eventually made it to his feet with some help but it was not clear just what his injury was. It did not look too serious, certainly not as serious at the injury sustained by Pryce, because Lolohea, whose face had ironically adorned the cover of the match-day programme, made his way off the pitch without the need of a stretcher. Yet it turned out to be anything but. A few days later, a statement released by Quins revealed the shocking truth. Not only had Lolohea broken the thigh bone in his left leg, he had also broken and dislocated a hip. He had needed five hours of surgery to repair the damage and would spend the next three months in a wheelchair. It was not just a season-ending injury, it was a career-threatening one.

The loss of Lolohea, tragic as it was, failed to knock Quins out of their stride against Castleford. Leading 18-4 at the break, the home side made it 24-4 when hooker Chad Randall dived over for a fourth try, converted by Henry Paul. The Tigers reduced the deficit with tries for Craig Huby and Gray Viane, but Quins had the win they desperately needed and Rea had the perfect send-off he so richly deserved.

In the after-match press conference, Rea was joined by directors Lenagan, David Hughes and Gerry Bouman. Media manager Chris Warren was also in attendance to make sure the next few minutes went as smoothly as possible. The assembled newspaper and radio journalists packed into the press room in the heart of the Lexus Stand wanted to know what was happening to Rea. More importantly, they wanted official confirmation that Brian McDermott was taking over. But they had to wait a few minutes more as Rea started by answering questions about the match. He was delighted with the passion and commitment shown by his players, in particular McLinden, Paul and Daniel Heckenberg, and he was happy the club's plight had been eased with only their fourth home win in Super League XI.

Then came the announcement everyone had been waiting for. Rea was indeed standing down as coach and, yes, McDermott was taking his place. But Lenagan insisted it was not a "knee-jerk reaction" to the club's parlous position in the table. "Tony and I have been planning this re-structuring for some time," he revealed. The chairman admitted he had originally intended the change to happen once the season was over but felt it was in the club's best interests to implement it now. "Brian's the best young coach in Super League and is a great acquisition," he added. "We believe he is fully ready to make the step up to become a head coach."

Rea seemed genuinely comfortable with the announcement, which went some way to answering the question everyone wanted to ask: Had he been forced out against his will? In the King's Bar afterwards, he was given a rousing send-off by the fans. His relationship with the club's supporters has not always been smooth. Calls for his dismissal were a constant backdrop to his six years in charge and he deliberately avoided becoming too close to them. "I have so much admiration for all our fans, the way they go up north to support us," said Rea. "I love them to death. I want them to have a rapport with the players so that's why I tended to distance myself from them."

Rea felt he could look back on his reign with a great deal of pride and that he had made a positive contribution. "I think every player who has come here has been heaps better for it," he said. "All the staff have gone on to good jobs and the players have maximised themselves, often playing their best footy with us. I like to think we have done a good job with them."

The end of Rea's reign coincided with McLinden's 27th birthday. The skipper's mother and sister had come over from Australia for the game and were clearly revelling in his popularity with the supporters. There was plenty of banter going on, too. When McLinden's mum suggested it would not be long before her son was back home where he belonged, Warren wasted little time in pointing out to her that the former Canberra Raiders star had recently signed a new three-year contract.

Most of the squad were heading out to belatedly celebrate Thomas Leuluai's 21st birthday. There was a definite party atmosphere about the place and the players were in a mood to celebrate. The chapter had closed on Rea's tenure as head coach but life moved on.

Behind the scenes at The Twickenham Stoop

Brian McDermott and Tony Rea watch from high in the Lexus Stand. (Photo: Peter Lush)

Above left: Dr Dee Jennings, the club's long-serving doctor. (Photo: Peter Lush)

Above right: Kitman Steve McGee, who has been involved with the club from the very start. Behind Steve is Dominic Fenton, the club's football operations manager. (Photo: Philip Gordos)

10. The life of Brian

"If you chopped me in half, you would find the Royal Marines with a little bit of the Bradford Bulls."
Brian McDermott, new Harlequins RL coach

Brian McDermott felt very much like the new boy at school as he prepared to meet his players for the first time as head coach of Harlequins RL. It was 8.30am on Monday, two days after Quins had won Tony Rea's last game at the helm. McDermott had thought long and hard over the weekend about what he was going to say. "It was the big one – first impressions last," he said. "You have lots of chances to make amends for any wrong words in that first meeting, but you don't want to make it difficult for yourself."

A few days earlier, McDermott had addressed another group of players, but with a very different agenda. After almost two seasons as a coach with Leeds Rhinos, initially in charge of the junior academy side and then as assistant to first-team boss Tony Smith, he had decided to leave to try his hand as a head coach in his own right. After helping Leeds become Super League champions in 2004 and then reach the Grand Final and final of the Challenge Cup the following year, McDermott had naturally grown attached to the players at Headingley. "Telling them I was going was pretty emotional," said McDermott. At least he left on a winning note. In his final game with the Rhinos they beat fierce rivals Bradford, the team McDermott had served so loyally as a player for 10 years.

McDermott had been offered the chance to take over at Quins just two days before that Friday night game against the Bulls. He had been in talks with the London club for several months about taking over at the end of the season but had suddenly been told he was wanted sooner rather than later - a lot sooner. The development caught McDermott off guard and ensured the former prop endured a couple of sleepless nights. He knew that accepting the job with Quins would mean leaving his comfort zone. He had a very good position at Leeds and his family had recently moved to a new house in North Yorkshire. But he also knew that opportunities like this did not come along very often. He came to a decision. He would accept the challenge of leading Harlequins RL.

It was midway through 2005 that McDermott had started to think it was time to move from under the wing of Smith, the man who had given him his first big coaching job at Huddersfield Giants and then taken him to Leeds. After working under Karl Harrison with the England team at the end of that season, McDermott's confidence in his own abilities had increased and he set himself a target – to become head coach of a Super League club by the end of the following season. When Harlequins RL expressed an interest in his services at the start of 2006, he quickly realised that this was a club that had ambitions to match his own. More importantly, he thought the current squad had plenty of promise and could really make their mark.

"I had looked at them and thought they were the type of people I would be proud to coach," he said. "They had bags of skill and didn't mind throwing the ball about. I thought that if you could combine that expressiveness with some tough, uncompromising play, then it made for an exciting team." But McDermott anticipated taking over at the end of the season, not with eight games still to go. He was keen to take a break once the current campaign was over so he could recharge his batteries and spend some time with his family.

His involvement with England the previous winter had meant that he had effectively coached for two seasons without a break. But when Quins invited him to take over in early July, his plans for some rest and recuperation went out of the window. Instead, he had a decision to make – and he made it quickly, agreeing to succeed Rea once Quins had played Castleford. "I saw it as taking charge of my own destiny," he said. "I didn't want to be sitting around twiddling my thumbs hoping Harlequins would still be interested in me at the end of the year, so I decided to accept the challenge."

As the Quins players assembled in front of him for the first time on the Monday after the win over Castleford, McDermott was anxious to get off on the right foot. "At the time I thought bollocks to this, I'll just speak from the heart," he said. "So I told the players there would be no Winston Churchill-type speech or 40 minute lecture about who I was and what I was about. I said they would work that out for themselves soon enough. I just introduced myself, told them they should give Tony Rea the respect he was due, but that I was in charge now and they would be sick of my voice within three days."

Hard work is at the very core of McDermott. It is something he trusts in and has helped him overcome the disappointments and setbacks he has suffered in his life. On more than one occasion he has been given the kind of news that might have finished someone less determined. Each time, he simply worked harder and harder until he proved himself.

McDermott was born in Wakefield, a town with a rich rugby league heritage. It used to be coal-mining country and the people are bred tough, well suited to such a brutal game. Children are as likely, if not more likely, to play rugby league than football. All of McDermott's seven brothers played the game at some stage. Paul turned out for both Wakefield and Sheffield Eagles while another two were on professional contracts at some point during their careers. Brian insists he was far from the most talented of the siblings and had stopped playing by the age of 13 or 14. Instead, he wanted to be a soldier, in particular a Royal Marine, and pursued his goal as soon as he left school.

By 17 he had made it, spending the next five years in the service of Her Majesty. He was mainly based in Arbroath but travelled extensively. "I ran about the world a little bit, did a bit of this and a bit of that," he said. "I thoroughly enjoyed it and would not do anything different if I had my time again." Life in the Marines suited McDermott down to the ground. He enjoyed pushing his body and mind to the limit and loved the comradeship that a life in the military offered. He also got to indulge his other passion, boxing, losing just two of his 25 fights as an amateur super-heavyweight. "Everything I have today I owe to the Marines," he said. "The things I learnt are what I base myself upon. The ethos of who you are and how to conduct yourself – that is what I draw everything from. If you chopped me in half, you would find the Royal Marines with a little bit of the Bradford Bulls."

In 1989, McDermott was posted to the Royal Marine School of Music at Deal in Kent. On 22 September an IRA bomb devastated the recreation room, killing 11 people and injuring many others. The blast could be heard in a village almost two miles away. According to McDermott, security "went through the roof" and he was assigned to guard duty. He found standing in front of a gate for hours at a time a largely mundane task. But at least he was able to look forward to a week off every fortnight. He often returned home to Wakefield when he had some spare time. It was while he was back in his home town that he started playing rugby league again, turning out for the Eastmoor Dragons team he had played for as a youngster. He was eventually spotted by a scout from Bradford Northern and asked to play in a trial game. He impressed and was offered a contract. "They signed me on for something like three pence over three years," recalled McDermott. "I was a bit of a filler. They needed some bodies." He now had a decision to make. The Marines had given him so much, yet here was an unexpected chance to make a go of it in rugby league. It was an opportunity he was reluctant to let pass. He took the plunge and quit the military.

McDermott was extremely fit thanks to his boxing - probably fitter than most of his new team-mates at Bradford. Yet he had hardly played rugby league since his early teens and was way behind in the skills stakes. If he was going to catch up, he had plenty of work to do on his tackling, catching and passing. But then hard work was something he relished. "When I first started at Bradford, people were always wondering whether I would make it or not," he said. "I always felt I had to fight tooth and nail to get a first-team game. When I did get a game, I felt like I had to fight tooth and nail to keep my place." Peter Fox eventually handed him his debut towards the end of the 1992-93 season and continued to show faith in the young prop until his departure in 1995. But then things changed dramatically for McDermott.

He thought the subsequent appointment of new coach Brian Smith would be good news for him. "I thought here we go, here is a coach who will appreciate that I am fit and can run all day," remembered McDermott. How wrong he was. Smith, an Australian who had coached South Sydney Rabbitohs, Hull FC and St George, dropped a bombshell by telling the former Marine he was not good enough and advised him to quit and get a job. "The first thing he said to me was that I could leave if I wanted," said McDermott, who drove back to Wakefield in tears. "I was devastated. I thought I was tough because I had been in the Marines for five years but I felt as though my life has just collapsed around me and my whole dream was finished."

It is an experience McDermott has not forgotten. As Harlequins RL head coach, he knows he will have to deliver similar news to players he has decided are not for him. "When I sit a player down in front of me, I'm very mindful of that, probably too mindful," he said. "It is something that I might need to toughen up on. It hits you hard when you explain to a player that he is not going to be kept and they more or less plead with you to change your mind. I suppose you have to be hard-nosed about some decisions. If you aren't, then you end up being a mediocre club."

When Smith broke the bad news to him, McDermott already had a job, working as a plasterer's assistant for his dad. But he knew that if he was going to prove Smith wrong and carve out a career for himself as a professional rugby league player, he needed to train every day, just like the professionals. Smith agreed to let McDermott stay on but made it clear the club could not offer him any money. Undeterred, McDermott seized the opportunity with both hands and gave up his job. "I just worked really hard and everything he asked for I did twice as much," said McDermott. "If he wanted me to jump high, I tried to jump higher. I was desperate to play but I was skint and knew that this was my last crack at it."

McDermott trained with a fiery intensity week after week, month after month. He did so because he felt he had to. "It is a bit like those old boxers, the likes of Jake La Motta," he said. "They were not nasty people by choice, they were nasty because they had to be, because there was nothing else in the world for them. I did not want to go out and work, I wanted to play rugby league." The blood, sweat and tears eventually paid off.

In the closing months of 1995, McDermott got his chance. Bradford were due to play at Warrington but several players had been struck down with illness, so Smith called in the reserves. McDermott found himself in a Bradford shirt again, alongside several trialists, and was determined to seize his unexpected chance. He did just that, helping a weakened Bradford side pull off a memorable win. As he trooped off the pitch at the end of the game, a delighted Smith shook him warmly by the hand and told him he had earned himself a contract. "The pressure I was feeling – that if I make a mess of this I might be gone – it was not a nice way to play," said McDermott. "The shock of earning a contract soon turned into elation. I thought 'hey I'm going to get paid, I'll have some money' but there was also a feeling that it was not before time. I had really put it in and had started to wonder how many more times I would have to prove myself."

McDermott spent his first week in charge of Harlequins RL living in a hotel on one side of Richmond Park. He missed his family, who remained in Yorkshire while he searched for a new family home, but he knew it was only a temporary situation. "I kept thinking this is hard, not being with my family, but then I'd see a piece on the news about someone who has been run over or somebody who had been murdered and I'd give myself a kick up the arse."

He had never found it difficult to switch off as a player, but this was different. He had so much on his mind that he found it difficult to sleep. "For the first couple of days I was going back to the hotel and thinking 'I'd like to be able to do this and I'd like to be able to do that'. I was thinking about the plans for the following day, thinking about the staff and thinking about what needed doing." There was also a more fundamental problem he needed to address. The sizeable contingent of players from the southern hemisphere was finding it difficult to understand his broad Yorkshire accent. He would either have to persist and hope they eventually caught on, or develop some other way of communicating with them.

McDermott's first few days in charge passed in a blur. In what seemed like no time at all, his first game as coach of Harlequins RL was upon him and it could not have been a more difficult assignment. St Helens had shown ruthless efficiency in beating

Quins 40-16 on the opening weekend of Super League XI and beat them again 16-6 at Knowsley Road in April. Now, as they prepared to welcome the London side for a second time in 2006, they were sitting pretty at the top of the table, having lost just three times all season, and were through to the semi-finals of the Challenge Cup. Quins, in contrast, had lost 12 of their 20 games and sat seventh in the table, perched just three points above Wigan. Not that his side's precarious position was McDermott's prime concern. He had spent his first week in charge working on a game plan. Above all, he wanted to see evidence that his players were at least trying to implement what he asked of them. "If they didn't, then I knew I would have to resell what I was trying to give to them," he said. "I could not have given a toss about the result."

St Helens proved too strong for their opponents, winning 30-24, but it was a competitive encounter. Daniel Heckenberg scored a try for the visitors with barely 90 seconds on the clock and Henry Paul added the conversion to make it 6-0. The home side looked nervous and made a series of handling errors. Paul extended the lead with a penalty after 11 minutes before the Saints machine finally clicked into gear. By half-time, the league leaders were 18-8 up and apparently cruising to victory. But second-half scores from Tyrone Smith and Mark McLinden hauled Quins back into it and ensured Daniel Anderson's side were made to work hard for the entire 80 minutes before sealing yet another win.

McDermott detected some despondency in the Quins dressing room after the game. He was fairly satisfied with their efforts, and pleased they had tried to execute the game plan he had given them. But he sensed they felt let down. He had been billed as their saviour, the man to lead them to safety, yet he had failed to come up with a winning formula in his first game. McDermott was not despondent, though. He knew there would be no instant fix. He simply told his players to turn up to training on Monday morning determined to work hard and with a smile on their faces.

Back in 1995 when he had finally earned a full-time contract with Bradford under Brian Smith, McDermott was not about rest on his laurels. He quickly established himself in the first team and went on to enjoy a very successful playing career. The prop won three Grand Finals and made four appearances for Great Britain, playing his part in a memorable victory over Australia at Old Trafford in November 1997. "It does not get better than beating the Aussies," he said. "I suppose that a few years earlier I had been patrolling the streets of Northern Ireland with the Marines." But trophies and accolades meant little to McDermott. "I don't put much worth on silverware," he said. "But if I had a trophy to signify that I had made a career out of rugby league, then that would be the one on the mantelpiece."

What McDermott loved most about rugby league was being part of a team, bonding with his colleagues and collecting memories he will carry with him forever. "I think back to the training sessions we used to have, the mates I made – they are the success stories," he said. "Sometimes you put your body in places where it hurts for a team-mate and that forms a bond that cannot be broken. There will always be that understanding between players on the same team. We might not go round to each other's houses very often anymore but there will always be that bond between us." McDermott's playing career finally ended with Bradford's Grand Final defeat at the hands of St Helens in 2002. It was a cruel loss, Sean Long kicking a last-minute drop-goal to give Saints a 19-18 victory in a dramatic game at Old Trafford. "I had to stop because my body was buggered," said McDermott. "I didn't miss the contact stuff, but what I did miss was the comradeship, looking into each other's eyes and knowing that we had done a good job."

By the time he decided to hang up his boots, McDermott had already begun thinking about life after playing. He had started helping out the coach of Eastmoor Dragons under-11s team in 1997, teaching them the basics and giving them the benefit of his wisdom. He really enjoyed it. "I made some errors that make me cringe when I look back," said McDermott, who coached the same bunch of youngsters as they progressed through the age groups. "I used to flog them and they loved it at the time, but that is not always the best way to get results. That was a massive lesson for me. I learnt more from those kids than I did from Brian Smith." Some of what he learnt he still uses. "Some of the sessions with Harlequins have been exactly the same as those I did with Eastmoor under-11s," he added. "The basics, the ethics, the core skills bit – nothing changes."

The brutal honesty of the kids he dealt with at Eastmoor was a chastening experience for McDermott, but he thinks it gave him a head start on his peers when it came to starting out as a coach. "To stand up and speak to a group of people of any age is daunting but more so with kids," he said. "They pull faces when you speak and will tell you if you have odd socks on." What's more, McDermott found coaching a team comprised of many single-parent and under-privileged children very humbling. "We had a player who had to walk the four miles to the training ground because he could not afford the bus fare," said McDermott. "I thought that sort of thing had died out in the 1930s. He was the bloke who kept my feet on the ground whenever I was in danger of getting too big for my boots."

McDermott acknowledges his time with Eastmoor helped prepare him for a life in coaching once his playing days were over. When reflecting on his spell as assistant coach of the Dragons, he leans forward a little in his seat and speaks with a genuine warmth and affection for the young men he worked with. It is not because they won any silverware - they never did - but because they made the most of what they had through hard work. "I remember things that went on in that team that will stay with me for a long time," he said. "There was a kid who was called 'The Brick' because he was shaped like one. He had something wrong with his hip and could not run properly. He used to play prop and still plays now. There was another player who could hardly see anything through his jam-jar glasses. I hope those kids look back on their time with Eastmoor and think that they were good days, just like I do when I think about my time with the Bulls."

One of the big things McDermott learned at Eastmoor was that you can ask too much of players. It was a trap he was keen to avoid falling into in his first few days as head coach of Harlequins RL. With the team still in need of points to ease their relegation worries, the last thing he wanted to do was bamboozle them. "Players tend to take a step back when you throw something new at them," said McDermott. "For instance, David Mills likes to run over the top of people when he is going forward and then break them in two when they run at him. We think he is capable of more and we want to add a few more strings to his bow, but we are only going to do that in pre-season. If I started doing it now, I would lose a bit of what he's good at, and I cannot afford to do that."

However, McDermott issued a clear mandate of what lay ahead for his players as he prepared his team for the visit of in-form Hull FC, only his second game at the helm. "When pre-season starts, we are going to break their bodies in two and build them up again," he said. "You have to kill them to make them come alive again."

McDermott owes a great deal of gratitude to Tony Smith for helping him make the transition from wannabe head coach into the real deal. Smith, younger brother of former Bradford boss Brian Smith, saw enough in McDermott to make him his assistant at Huddersfield Giants and then take him to Leeds Rhinos. Under Smith, McDermott says his "learning curve went through the roof" and he believes there is no better head coach for an assistant to work under. "I will always be thankful for what Tony did," said McDermott. "It is quite easy as a head coach to just go about your business and let the assistant pick up the pieces and while giving them nothing back. Tony went above and beyond."

The most important thing McDermott learnt from his former boss was making sure the players took to the field in the right frame of mind. Once a game has started, a coach wields little influence from the sidelines. Good communication is also key. If players fail to follow a gameplan or a drill breaks down in training, McDermott says that the probable cause is a lack of clarity from the coach. Working for Smith, McDermott also discovered that the job of head coach involves so much more than simply training and playing. There are staff briefings, video sessions, press conferences, club functions and a host of other things to deal with. It can be gruelling at times. Game day often comes as a release.

Hull FC arrived at the Twickenham Stoop on 22 July looking to extend their unbeaten run to 14 games. Peter Sharp's side were third in the table and breathing down the neck of second-placed Leeds. But they were taking on Harlequins RL without several key players, notably Paul Cooke, Kirk Yeaman and Richard Whiting, and soon found themselves behind. Quins skipper Mark McLinden showed why he is one of the most exciting players in the British game by scoring in the very first minute. He collected a chip from Hull's Sid Domic before scything his way through the opposition defence for an 85-yard try. It was a scintillating score, but offered only a glimpse of what was to come from the Australian full-back.

Kirk Dixon kicked a penalty for Hull before two handling errors from Nick Bradley-Qalilawa put the Quins defence under severe pressure. Earlier in the season the home side may well have crumbled, but they showed tremendous grit and determination to keep the visitors at bay. Their resilience was rewarded when McLinden grabbed his second try of the game following a superb break from Thomas Leuluai. With three minutes of the first half left, McLinden then executed a bewildering series of sidesteps and dummies to complete a stunning hat-trick. The score helped Quins open up an 18-2 lead at the break and prompted warm applause from the home fans as their team left the field.

If the first half belonged to the skipper, it is doubtful whether he remembered anything of the second 40 minutes. In making a courageous last-ditch clearance just after the interval, he sustained a blow to the head that left him sprawled out in his own in-goal area. As he was assisted from the field, a radio commentator from Hull quipped on air: "He's a spaceman at the moment, he does not know whether he is on this planet or Venus." McLinden's importance to Quins cannot be underestimated. So it came as no surprise when Hull took advantage of his absence to score two tries and move within eight points of their hosts with 19 minutes remaining. Quins were hanging on, but they managed to stop the visitors from crossing again until the very last minute. Nathan

Hull fall to McLinden's magic

Mark McLinden scores the first of his hat-trick of tries.

The Quins defence was also at its best in the first half against in-form Hull.

Quins celebrate another McLinden try. (All photos: Peter Lush)

Rob Purdham shared the kicking duties with Henry Paul, converting two of McLinden's tries.

Jon Wells being tackled. Quins failed to score after the break and held on for a narrow 18-16 victory against a Hull side chasing their 14th successive win. (Photos: Peter Lush).

Blacklock's try and Kirk Dixon's conversion closed the gap to just two points. But it proved sufficient for the home side. Hull ran the ball as the hooter went, keeping it alive for what was an agonising length of time, but Daniel Heckenberg eventually fell on the ball, to loud cheers from the Quins contingent.

The 18-16 victory over Hull gave Harlequins RL some valuable breathing space in the battle to avoid relegation from Super League. It also breathed new life into their struggle to make the play-offs. McDermott was certainly in upbeat mood when he faced the media after the game. "It is such a good feeling to get my first win with the club," he said. "We knew Hull weren't going to go down easily and we died on our arses in the second half. But the victory was down to the team's desire and desperation. There are still lots of points to play for." Looking back on the win over Hull several weeks later, McDermott described it as a bonus. "I was possibly willing to accept another defeat," he said. But he was under no illusions about the size of the task facing him, especially given the way his team had collapsed in the second half. At least he knew what was required - a lot of hard work.

11. The man at the top

"We got some things wrong, but then in the first year of change you always get some things wrong. We will get a lot less wrong next year."
Ian Lenagan, Harlequins RL chairman and joint owner

Wander through the King's Bar at the Twickenham Stoop after a game and you will generally see him somewhere, perhaps a pint of bitter in one hand, more often than not discussing the match or some aspect of the club with a supporter. The suit is a bit of a giveaway, sets him apart from the average Harlequins RL fan on match day. But then again there is nothing average about Ian Lenagan. A multi-millionaire businessman, Lenagan is the largest shareholder in WorkPlace Systems, the computer company he built from scratch and the business that is the source of much of his wealth. He is also heavily involved with the Sports Cafe chain and is the man behind a string of theatre productions in the West End of London. His highly impressive curriculum vitae also tells you he is a former Mayor of the Oxfordshire village of Woodstock, the birth place of Sir Winston Churchill. He also has interests in several pubs around the county and backs countless charities and organisations. Lenagan, a man of many roles, is also the chairman and joint owner of Harlequins RL.

Spend a few moments in Lenagan's company and it becomes clear that his knowledge and understanding of rugby league are considerable. Born in 1946 into a working class family in the Wigan parish of St Patricks, his love of the game – and Wigan in particular - began at an early age thanks to his grandfather. Tom Moran was passionate about Wigan, so passionate that he took all 11 of his grandchildren at formative times in their lives to the Hen Pen at Central Park to cheer them on. He thought that if he took each of them three times they would either be hooked on rugby league for life or decide that the game was simply not for them. It seemed like sound logic. Lenagan fell into the former category and, like most of the other grandchildren, has been a Wigan fan ever since. That much is evident from walking into his Milton Keynes office, where the influence of the Cherry and Whites on his life is unmistakable. On one wall there is a picture of Martin Offiah scoring his famous length-of-the field try in the 1994 Challenge Cup Final win over Leeds at Wembley. Several feet away is a painting of Ellery Hanley, Shaun Edwards and Dean Bell, the three Wigan captains during the club's historic run of eight successive Challenge Cup triumphs. Lenagan has witnessed most of Wigan's glorious moments in person, including the World Club Championship victory over Brisbane in 1994. He was one of just 150 away supporters at the ANZ Stadium to see his side record a shock 20-14 win over the Broncos. "I flew in, watched the match and flew out the next day," he said. "It was a dreadful journey but worth it for the game."

For a long time, Lenagan was content being just a rugby league supporter. He had dreamed of owning Wigan but knew that was never going to become reality. As for investing in another club, well, that was tantamount to treason in his view. He had met the directors of one Yorkshire club several years back and got to know them well. But his loyalty to Wigan prevented him from taking the next step and digging deep into his pocket. It was only when he was approached about taking an active involvement in the London Broncos at the start of 2005 that he began to entertain the idea of nailing his colours to another mast. He was keen for the game to flourish in the capital and felt he could make a telling difference. "Putting something into London was a good way of doing something for the game because I honestly believe that London and France are a critical element of rugby league being successful," he said. However, he was not about to make a snap decision and thought "long and hard" before agreeing to invest in the club. First and foremost, he wanted assurances from current owner David Hughes that his money and expertise would be welcomed. "David had been the saviour of the Broncos for years," said Lenagan. "I needed to be persuaded that he would not mind me taking over." Hughes, who had made his money from the oil trade, made it abundantly clear that any concerns Lenagan had were unfounded, that his business acumen was desperately required. "David said to me 'I'm an oil trader and successful at that, but marketing, finance, business management, human resources etc are not my strengths'." Having been given the green light by Hughes, Lenagan proceeded to go over the club's accounts with a fine tooth comb. Once that process was complete, he knew exactly what he was getting involved with. However, there was still one stronger, more emotional consideration that had to be resolved before he could commit himself 100 per cent.

Lenagan still needed to know his love for Wigan would not prevent him from feeling passionate towards another club. If he could not get enthusiastic about the Broncos, then he felt it was pointless investing large amounts of his time and money. The pivotal moment came during the club's on-the-road game against Leeds Rhinos in the south of France. The match at Perpignan's Stade Aime Giral on 9 July 2005 could not have gone much better as far as the Broncos were concerned. Up against a Leeds side who sat on top of the Super League table, they ran in six tries in a shock

32-24 victory. "I actually found myself shouting and supporting the Broncos," said Lenagan, one of 7,000 spectators inside the ground. "I always said that if I got to that point I would do it, I would invest in the club."

London went on to finish the 2005 season in the sixth and final play-off spot, edging out Wigan in the process. But their hopes of further progress were dashed by eventual champions Bradford, who thumped them 44-22 at Odsal. Lenagan had made his commitment to the Broncos official by this point, agreeing to become the new chairman and majority shareholder with 65 per cent of the shares. But if he thought the club would reproduce their 2005 achievement in 2006, or hopefully better it, then he was to be disappointed. By the time Harlequins RL, as the Broncos were now known, travelled to The Willows on Friday 4 August, they were more worried about relegation than a top-six spot. The play-offs were not out of reach, but realistically they needed to beat Salford on their own patch then beat them again at the Stoop on the final weekend of the regular season. The significance of the encounters against Karl Harrison's team was obvious. The Reds occupied sixth place while Quins sat three places and three points below them. Win both games against Salford and Quins would give themselves a shot at overhauling their opponents.

Brian McDermott's team had beaten in-form Hull in their last game while Salford had suffered a poor 26-6 reverse at Catalans Dragons. Factor in a 29-28 win for the Quins at The Willows back in May and there was considerable optimism in the London camp. It proved to be woefully misplaced. Quins had been blanked earlier in the season, thrashed 60-0 at home to Leeds. But few expected a whitewashing by Salford. It was supposed to be a competitive fixture between two teams with genuine play-off aspirations, but Salford's Luke Robinson inspired his team to a 34-0 win with a superb display of scrum-half skills. The former Wigan player somehow eluded a two-man tackle to score a try just before the break, but his contribution constituted so much more than those four points. He was at the heart of his side's attacking manoeuvres time and again as Quins were run ragged. It was a chastening experience for the visiting coach, who admitted some weeks later that the loss had shown him just how much he had to do. "There was going to be no more pussy-footing around after that," said McDermott. "I knew I had just five more games to turn things around."

Lenagan is an intelligent, articulate man. Ask him a complicated, multi-faceted question and he will quickly formulate a coherent, well-ordered answer. His words are calculated and precise. He often precedes an answer by posing a question, as if to specifically underline the point he is making. Although not a tall man, he undoubtedly has gravitas while his words convey belief and purpose. With his ability to disseminate information allied with the clarity of his thinking, it is easy to imagine him operating in the boardrooms of his businesses or the institutions of the City. Yet his success is no accident.

Awarded a scholarship through the 11 plus system, Lenagan, with no Catholic grammar school in Wigan at the time, was educated at West Park in St Helens. He was keen on rugby, pulling on his union jersey on a Saturday and his league one on a Sunday. He played stand-off or hooker and had his nose broken twice. He was eventually warned off the game by a wise, old prop, who advised the young Lenagan to stick with union and make the most of the opportunities a grammar school education would offer him. The forward, whose livelihood depended on the game, made it clear that he would have no hesitation in smashing Lenagan if it made him look good.

Lenagan studied mathematics at Manchester University, gaining a BSc, before completing a Masters degree in Magnetohydrodynamics at Liverpool University. From there, he moved into scientific programming and worked for the Central Electricity Generating Board in Southwark, London. He was based in the building that now houses the Tate Modern art gallery, but soon became aware of the limitations of his choice. "Within 12 months I realised that there was no career path in this," he said. He began working for American company Burroughs Corporation, now Unisys, selling computer systems in Liverpool. On his first day with the company, Lenagan was dropped at the dock road in Bootle and told to report back only when he had sold one of the company's products, an old-fashioned adding machine. "It was not an easy environment," he said. "Success comes hard and there were many times when I wanted to quit." Despite his reservations, Lenagan stuck with the job and eventually became a branch manager in Leeds via spells in the United States, Switzerland and various other places. At 29, he was the company's youngest ever branch manager in the United Kingdom. He was also one of the best, transforming Leeds from a rundown unit into one of the most profitable.

Lenagan decided to take a break from computers in the 1980s and became managing director of Banbury Homes & Gardens. It was another important stage in his all-round business development. The company had five factories and were losing a lot of money. "I learned some harsh lessons," said Lenagan. "Having to close down factories, re-site manufacturing and change the product range... it is harsh, a harsh environment." But the experience armed him with yet more skills and gave him the confidence to start up his own business. He knew exactly what he was going to do. "I always said that if I worked for myself I would create systems for managing people in the workplace, so that you get quick feedback on productivity, performance, attendance and the usage of people," he said. Working for Banbury Homes & Gardens, Lenagan had been frustrated at not being able to find out whether any changes he implemented had worked until the payroll came out, roughly eight weeks later. He was determined to come up with a way of speeding the whole process up. So, after selling his red BMW 525e to raise the necessary funds, he set about achieving his goal, renting out a 1000 square foot office two miles from his current headquarters in Milton Keynes and giving himself 10 weeks to design a product and get paid for it. He spent two weeks on his own designing the first system. Then, after hiring a programmer, he tested it, refined it and finally managed to sell it. Lenagan was up and running.

WorkPlace Systems proved to be extremely successful. Lenagan had identified a gap in the market and filled it. "I never took a bank loan or an overdraft," he said. "I always said I would never do that. The whole business is built on self-generated profit. It floated in 2000 at a very high value. The figures are confidential but I sold 11 per cent and got £29m." His fortune was estimated at £182 million by *The Sunday Times* in 2001, putting him at 182nd on their Rich List that year. The newspaper also chose to put a photograph of the BMW he had sold to start his company on the front page of their business section. But Lenagan kept his feet firmly on the ground. He even chose to give £12m of his fortune to family and friends. "What the hell," he said, "am I going to do with that amount of money?"

After the shocking loss to Salford, Harlequins RL knew their hopes of a play-off place had taken a major hit. Attempting to repair the damage would be a big job, not made any easier by the fact that Bradford were their next opponents. Quins had drawn 18-18 with the Bulls at Odsal back in February but had been crushed 58-16 at the Stoop in May. Now the reigning Super League champions were heading back to west London buoyed by a run of three successive wins, the last of which was a thumping 50-22 defeat of Warrington. The game against Bradford on Saturday, 11 August had special connotations for Quins coach Brian McDermott. He had spent 10 successful years with the club, helping them win three Grand Finals. Not only that, the Bulls were now coached by Steve McNamara, a good friend and former team-mate who had taken charge following Brian Noble's move to Wigan. Their first meeting as head coaches was ultimately to belong to McDermott, but, as seemed to be the way with Quins, victory was far from straightforward. Early tries for Lesley Vainikolo and Marcus Bai gave the visitors an 8-0 lead before Chad Randall wrong-footed the Bradford defence to score and give Quins hope. Shontayne Hape crossed for another Bulls try, but a 90-metre intercept score from Luke Dorn and a try from Lee Hopkins swung the match very much in home side's favour. Randall crossed again before the break, Henry Paul converting, to give Quins a 22-14 lead, which became 26-14 when Tyrone Smith scored immediately after the restart. Once again, though, Quins failed to press home their winning position. Paul Deacon scored for Bradford, converting his own try, before Paul kicked a penalty for Quins after the Bulls were punished for a high shot on Neil Budworth. Those two points proved crucial. Brett Ferres scored Bradford's fifth try, converted by Deacon, to make it 28-26. But despite 20 minutes still to go, Quins held on for their third home win on the trot.

Paul had shown all of his experience in the game against his former club. He seemed to be engaged in regular dialogue with the referee and could often be seen holding both hands up at the official, all 10 fingers indicating that the Bulls were offside. It was a deliberate tactic and one that McDermott would have appreciated. The Quins coach had nothing but praise for his former team-mate after the match. "We did not live in each other's pockets when we played together at Bradford but he has humbled me since I've been here," said McDermott. "I did not know how he would react to me as coach but he has been superb." McDermott also admitted it was satisfying to have put one over McNamara but asked the media not to concentrate too much on that individual duel. Instead, McDermott preferred to focus attention on Paul Sykes. The player had suffered a serious kidney injury back in March and been told he would not play again in 2006. Yet here he was, throwing himself into tackles with such gusto that it beggared belief. Filling in at full-back in the absence of the injured Mark McLinden, his name was greeted by a cheer from the fans when it was read out before the match. Sykes went on to have a solid game, overcoming an early mistake when he failed to collect an awkward bouncing ball and allowed Bradford to score.

Sykes had not been permitted to do anything but rest for the first four months following his injury, sustained against Hull on 3 March. "I was just sitting at home in front of the computer," he said. "I went on a few weekends away but that was about it." His doctor eventually gave him permission to start light training once it became clear he was making a far quicker recovery than expected. Then, just five months after being told he had suffered an injury that may result in the loss of a kidney, he was back in action, playing in an under-21 match at Wigan. Next came the first-team clash against the Bulls, the club with whom Sykes started his career. "I was a bit nervous ahead of the game but more excited than anything else," he said. "To get through the whole 80 minutes was a bonus, I had not expected that." McDermott was impressed just like everyone else was. "Paul was massive for us," he said. "His willingness to do the unglamorous things was outstanding."

In the immediate aftermath of the victory over Bradford, the Quins players gathered in a huddle for a lengthy period of time before going over to thank their supporters. Chants of "We're Quins RL" had broken out during the closing stages of the match while one fan held aloft a George Cross flag with the same words written across the middle. Lenagan did not miss the significance of the moment. On the eve of the season, the chairman discussed his relationship with the supporters and what they thought of the transformation from London Broncos to Harlequins. "There is a 10 per cent minority that is completely antagonistic to any involvement with union," he said. "But I don't think there are many people that want it to fail." Lenagan felt most of the criticism revolved around the change of name. He had some "frank exchanges" with some supporters towards the end of the Broncos final season, but felt it was his duty as chairman to listen to what they had to say. He was not going to give them any flannel in return either. "The one thing that they know is that if I say something I say it in a direct manner, the way it is, without any spin," he said. "I cannot stand politics or any of that crap. I have no time for it in any of the businesses I am involved with." The chanting of 'We're Quins RL', which was also heard towards the end of the games against both Hull and Bradford, was one of the high points for Lenagan. It showed to him that the club's name - and the fears associated with the move to the Stoop - no longer seemed to be a major issue.

Not everything had run smoothly during the first season as Harlequins RL. The on-field inconsistencies had made the off-the-field task a lot more difficult. One of the first things Lenagan did prior to the start of the 2006 campaign was sit down with his management group and determine the best way of promoting the new venture. Chris Warren, the club's marketing and media manager, played a large part in the process. "The effort he put in nearly killed him," said Lenagan. "It was a fantastic effort. He was the creative force while I targeted the direction. We produced the whole of that campaign together."

Warren is most familiar to rugby league fans as the presenter of Sky's NRL coverage. The son of legendary Australian rugby league commentator Ray Warren, his pedigree is obvious. Yet he was also a decent player. He played a handful of first-grade games for Sydney's Western Suburbs in the NRL before moving to the ill-fated Western Reds, a new ARL franchise based in Perth. Warren was reserve-grade skipper for three seasons before injury eventually ended his career as a hooker in 1997. It was during his time in Sydney that he gained a degree in marketing and some valuable business experience with Pepsi Cola. He had then put his marketing skills to good use for the Reds, selling close to Aus$500,000 in advertising, hospitality and sponsorship packages in a city he did not know and situated far from the traditional league strongholds of Sydney and Brisbane. Despite his efforts, the Reds still incurred massive debts and were eventually axed at the end of 1997. Then after 18 months as marketing manager for Western Australia Tennis, Warren, like many an Australian before him, packed his rucksack and headed for London, initially dossing down with some mates he knew from his time at the Reds who were now earning a living with the Broncos.

Warren also explored the possibility of working for the Broncos in some kind of marketing role but was told by Tony Rea, chief executive at the time, that there were no vacancies and that the club did not want to be seen as employing too many Australians. A job with new Super League franchise Gateshead Thunder almost came off before Warren finally found employment with Sky. At the time, he was earning £4 an hour pulling pints and was only too happy to work for the satellite broadcaster, even if it meant just making cups of tea for Eddie Hemmings and Mike Stephenson. He thought he was being interviewed for a position in the marketing department but found himself in front of the cameras for a screen test. Before he knew it, he had been offered the job of presenting Sky's coverage of Australian rugby league. He was only too happy to accept. One month later, he received another job invitation, this time from the Broncos. Rea needed someone to fill a gap in the club's media department and thought Warren fitted the bill. Suddenly, he was a man in demand.

Upon joining the Broncos, then based at the Stoop, Warren soon realised the limitations of working for a club that continually struggled to balance the books. "We were based in a Portakabin out the back and had one computer to share between 10 people," he said. "I think we did pretty well considering it was very much a bare bones operation. We had a professional attitude, we just did not have the resources to go with it." That all changed when Lenagan came in and the club moved back to the Stoop. Now Warren and the rest of the marketing team are based in comfortable offices located in the bowels of the Lexus Stand.

Lenagan told Warren he wanted to sell Harlequins RL on the merits of rugby league, so the Australian went away and devised the marketing motto 'Speed, Power, Passion'. An advertising campaign followed to spread the message while the club's partnership with NEC Harlequins inevitably drew a substantial amount of media attention in its own right. As Lenagan remarked on the eve of the campaign: "Can any Broncos fan fail to be impressed with the amount of publicity that rugby league and the London club has achieved?"

The attendance of 8,213 for the opening game against St Helens vindicated the work done by Lenagan, Warren and the rest of the marketing team, but it soon became evident that there was more to life than a winning catchphrase. When Quins lost their next three home games, to Wakefield, Castleford and Leeds, the momentum and goodwill generated before the season quickly started to fade. "The lack of performance on the field in the first half of the season had a significant effect on the rest," said Lenagan. "It became clear quite quickly that the on-field performance was affecting our finances." Warren agreed. "You can shoot all your bullets, but they don't work in isolation," he said. "Everything has got to work in tandem. If you have a look at the attendance for game one we did arouse a lot of interest and a lot of people did come to have a look. Perhaps they weren't overly impressed with the product they trialled, but there is not a lot you can do about that."

Lenagan went into the season hoping to limit the loss to around £350,000 to £400,000 by the time it finished. He would cover 65 per cent of the costs and David Hughes would account for the remaining 35 per cent. But it soon became clear they would have to stump up more. It eventually emerged that a further £250,000 to £300,000 was required. Lenagan was undeterred. "That is what David and I are there for," he said. Nevertheless, attendances had been a little disappointing. Lenagan had been hopeful that, with a good start to the season allied to a successful marketing strategy, the club might average more than 4,000 in 2006. If they could achieve such a figure, it would minimise the deficit from his first season in charge. With season ticket sales for the first year back at the Stoop more than 60 per cent up on the previous year's figure of 700, he was optimistic too. But that early promise died away.

Lenagan quickly realised that Harlequins RL needed more of his attention than he first thought. He had anticipated devoting half a day a week on the club. But during the months leading up to the new season, he found he was spending two to two-a-half days a week on Quins, using up a lot of his evenings and weekends. There was to be no let-up either once the season was under way.

"Performances in the first half of the season meant we were distracted from the things we should have been concentrating on," he said.

A growing injury list did not help matters, but it also became evident that Quins were struggling to last the full 80 minutes. "Fitness was not what it should have been," reflected Lenagan. "The players died after 20 minutes of a match at the beginning of the season." Frenchman Thibault Giroud had been employed as the club's elite performance manager before the campaign began. His credentials were impressive. The French-born Tongan had run 100 metres in 10.53 seconds, played American football professionally for NFL Europe sides Munich Thunders, Barcelona Dragons and Amsterdam Admirals, and also competed in the 2002 Winter Olympics in the four-man bob. "Thibault is magnificent at speed and power, but not so experienced at the aerobic aspects of the stamina league players need," said Lenagan. "That was a management choice, not Thibault's fault." Nevertheless, Lenagan knew the issue of fitness would have to be addressed, if not during the season then after it. Hence the decision to replace Giroud once the 2006 campaign was over with former player Bill Peden. Since leaving the Broncos at the end of 2003, Peden had forged a name for himself in the fitness field, earning rave reviews for his work with the Newcastle Knights. His progress had not gone unnoticed back in London either. "Billy Peden was reputed to be the fittest man in rugby league," said Lenagan, who unveiled Peden's capture in July. "Because of his reputation in the NRL, we know he is going to get the players absolutely fit."

Peden was not the only high-profile capture in 2006. Both Lenagan and Tony Rea had been reluctant to make wholesale changes to the playing squad once the season had started, but then the chance to sign Henry Paul had presented itself. According to Lenagan, Paul's acquisition made "a mess" of the budget but he felt the former Wigan and Bradford player was a worthwhile investment. "Thank God we got him," said Lenagan. "It sent a message that we were serious. I have no regrets, but it was a straight addition to cost." There was also the arrival of McDermott as head coach at the start of July. Lenagan was impressed with Rea's achievements and still had faith in his ability to lead the first team, but both men felt it was time for a change. "Tony is a magnificent visionary, but after 10 years of looking at the same landscape it is very difficult to be perceptive," said Lenagan. "He cannot see the wood for the trees sometimes." Lenagan spoke to Wigan legends Shaun Edwards and Andy Farrell about the possible appointment of McDermott. He was keen to get their input on such an important matter.

What they told him remains private, but Lenagan says the extra money it cost to bring McDermott to the club was worth it. "I think Brian will be Great Britain coach in five years time, I don't have any doubt about that," said the chairman.

There were other unforeseen costs for Lenagan and Hughes. It was clear that hospitality had not generated the anticipated revenue. The sale of corporate boxes had exceeded expectations. Going into the campaign, the club had budgeted for the sale of five boxes, hoping they might reach 10. They ended up selling 23. A big success in the eyes of the chairman, yet not quite as significant as it might have been. In virtually all respects - merchandising, drink and ticket sales - the profile of a rugby union fan is similar to that of a league supporter. What Lenagan and his team discovered was that they differ substantially in the revenue-rich area of food. "League people do not seem to want to eat as much in a formal environment as people in union do," said Lenagan. So while service costs remained high, the money generated did not match expectations. The pre-season budgets had been compiled in part using information from NEC Harlequins. "You could say we should have realised the profile of a league spectator and their willingness to spend on X, Y and Z is different," said Lenagan. "Well, we were not clever enough for that, so we didn't." As the season wore on, other unconsidered factors came to light. For example, the cost of running hospitality in the East Stand is substantially more than in the Lexus Stand. "When you do a budget for a new business – which is what Quins RL is - what can you go off? It is a guestimate," said Lenagan. "We got some things wrong, but then in the first year of change you always get some things wrong. We will get a lot less wrong next year."

The same logic can be applied to the marketing campaign. Warren was broadly happy with the decision to focus on growing the club's community base. Quins looked to build their brand by ensuring it had a presence in local schools and rugby clubs as well as advertising on local radio stations, newspapers and transport networks. But the Australian felt Quins had "only really scratched the surface in terms of exposing our brand and our product". Warren was especially keen to develop a high-street presence, but the club did not have the manpower to realise that particular goal. "With more resources and more staff next season, we can do a lot more," he said.

Lenagan was not at the Halliwell Jones Stadium on 19 August to watch his team's match against Warrington. It was only the second game of the season he had not attended in person. The other one he had missed was also against the Wolves, the home fixture on 10

June. But at least he was able to watch both encounters on television. Unfortunately, the second game did not make good viewing. It proved to be another frustrating afternoon – and one that suggested that avoiding relegation rather than making the play-offs was the chief aim for the rest of the season. From the moment Brent Grose intercepted a poor pass from Henry Paul after five minutes to set up Warrington's first try, scored by Chris Bridge, it became clear Quins were always going to struggle. By half-time, the home side led 22-6. Nick Bradley-Qalilawa pulled a try back for the visitors after the restart, but Martin Gleeson replied to restore Warrington's 16-point advantage. Bradley-Qalilawa scored again and Chad Randall also crossed to give Quins hope, but Warrington held on for a 28-22 victory. Quins were gutted and McDermott was left rueing another slow start.

The result at Warrington would have come as no surprise to those people who had followed the fortunes of Quins closely in 2006. With three wins and three defeats from their previous six games - in a sequence of lose one, win one - it was somehow inevitable they would lose at the Halliwell Jones Stadium. For Lenagan, the outcome only emphasised what he already knew, that plenty of work still lay ahead.

12. Thanks for the memories

"A lot of people who have never met me think I am this crazy lunatic... but once you get know me I am a nice guy."
Danny Williams, Harlequins RL player

Harlequins RL's Super League play-off dreams hung by a thread on the morning of Saturday, 2 September. The previous weekend's defeat to Warrington left them needing to win their three remaining games to have any chance of making the top six. They had not won three matches in a row all season, so it was mission impossible in many people's eyes. But there was hope. Warrington, who occupied sixth spot, were five points ahead of Quins, who lay in seventh place, but were unlikely to pick up any more. They had been crushed 54-16 by Leeds the night before and faced high-flying Hull FC and St Helens in their remaining two matches. So if Quins could beat Castleford, Wigan and Salford in quick succession, the final play-off berth would be theirs. That was the plan. The first task, though, was to beat Castleford at the Jungle.

The Tigers had looked safe from relegation back in mid-July but had suffered an alarming slump since recording a shock 31-30 victory over Leeds. After looking like possible play-off contenders, they had lost their next four games to slip from seventh to 10th in the table, just one point better off than Wakefield and Catalans Dragons. Therefore, the visit of Harlequins RL was just as important to them. Perhaps more so. Lose it and their chances of avoiding an instant return to the National League would take a serious hit.

Maybe the thought of a second relegation in just three seasons proved the difference between the two sides. Castleford certainly showed more fight than Quins, who never got into their stride. In fact, in a game screened live by Sky, they were way below their best. They were out-fought and out-thought from first hooter to last. Only a brief spell before half-time offered any real hope, when tries from Paul Sykes and Danny Williams put the visitors 12-10 up. Peter Lupton, a former London Broncos player, gave the Tigers the lead again before the break. Then Willie Manu and Adam Fletcher went over in the second half to seal the win. Just to rub salt into the wounds, prop Danny Sculthorpe popped over a drop goal to make the final score 27-12.

A few refereeing decisions had gone against Quins at Castleford, but coach Brian McDermott was not looking to point the finger of blame at the officials. Instead, he praised the home team for showing "a lot of emotion" and admitted his side had let themselves down. The Quins fans were starting to get worried, though. Their hopes of a top-six spot had been finally extinguished, but their chief concern now was avoiding the drop. One win would ensure they finished above Wakefield, but they faced a rejuvenated Wigan side before finishing their season with a game against Salford, who had already booked their place in the play-offs. At least both games were at The Stoop, but the nerves were starting to really jangle. Few people connected with Quins would have imagined such a nail-biting and potentially disastrous scenario back in February, when the new era had yet to begin and the play-offs were the chief target. Now it was all about survival. There were many supporters – and a few members of the media - who did not think Quins would win another game. If that happened and the unthinkable became reality, well, the consequences were not worth contemplating.

Luke Dorn had been one of the few success stories of an ultimately disappointing 2006 season for Harlequins RL. The Australian would go on to finish as the club's leading tryscorer for the year with 18, four more than skipper Mark McLinden. Yet the former Northern Eagles and Sydney Roosters half-back, who had also scored 24 tries in his debut season, had been told he was no longer needed. "I spoke to the club midway through the season because I wanted to know what was happening, if they were going to offer me another deal," said Dorn. "They told me they needed my quota spot and wouldn't be offering me a new contract. I was naturally disappointed, but I wasn't going to let it affect my performances. I asked for permission to speak to other clubs and a few were interested. Salford showed the most interest, so I agreed a two-year deal with them."

Harlequins RL had five quota spots in 2006, occupied by Dorn, McLinden, Chad Randall, Lee Hopkins and Mark Tookey. With that number falling to four in 2007 and then three in 2008, in line with most other Super League clubs, Quins knew it had to start making some tough choices. Tookey's decision to return to Australia accounted for the quota spot that was being lost, but the club still needed to free up another after signing Melbourne Storm stand-off Scott Hill. With McLinden, Randall and Hopkins still under contract, the axe fell on Dorn. "I don't think I could have done a great deal more," he said. "I've achieved the goals I set myself when I came over here. The hard thing for me to accept is being replaced by someone in my own position. I thought they would go after a forward." Dorn had indeed been a big hit in his two seasons with the club. His speed of thought, dazzling footwork and remarkable ability to score intercept tries on a regular basis made him a very dangerous player. He had also formed one third of the fabled Golden Triangle with McLinden and Thomas Leuluai. He would be sorely missed, no doubt about that, and no wonder Salford coach Karl Harrison had expressed great delight in signing him. "It's going to be sad to go," said Dorn, who lived in Surbiton with girlfriend Lauren, a biomechanist. "I'll miss the hustle and bustle of London and I've loved my time here. I've seen almost all the sights and I've made some good friends. But I'm going to enjoy living somewhere that's not so expensive."

Disappointed at being booted out, Dorn was still determined to leave Harlequins RL on a high note. He was genuinely excited for the club's future following the move to the Stoop and did not want relegation to wreck that. "Quins have the potential to be really big, as big as they want," he said. "It's a question of people in the right places making the right decisions. I'm confident we won't go down. The lads were really down after the defeat by Castleford, but we've got to take control of the situation and not rely on others doing us a favour. We have got ourselves into this position and it's up to us to get ourselves out of it."

Harlequins RL had two games to save themselves, but everyone – players, fans and management – did not want the survival bid to go down to the last match against Salford. That would be a nightmare scenario, the last thing anyone had envisaged when the season had kicked off. The focus, then, was on beating Wigan on Saturday 9 September. Do that - or at least avoid defeat – and the pressure would be off. That was not going to be an easy proposition. The Warriors would arrive at the Twickenham Stoop in good heart after a 38-16 defeat of the Bradford Bulls and would still have an outside shot at the play-offs despite a two-point penalty for breaching the salary cap. Many felt the punishment should have been more severe, but Wigan seemed satisfied. The points deduction had dented their hopes of a top-six spot, but the second-half of their season had been all about survival in any case. They had achieved their goal in some style, too, winning nine of their last 10 games to rocket up the table from bottom place. They would present a formidable challenge to Harlequins RL.

If Quins had looked lacklustre against Castleford the previous weekend, they looked anything but against Wigan. They tore into their opponents from the off and were 12-0 up inside 16 minutes. First, Hopkins jinked his way over the line for his side's first try of the afternoon. Then Solomon Haumono scythed his way through the Wigan defence to touch down under the posts. The Warriors were clearly second best but reduced the deficit immediately – and

Wigan beaten at The Stoop – Quins avoid the drop

Left: Brian Noble and Brian McDermott before the match
Right: Paul Sykes and Jon Wells watch from the sidelines.

Ready for battle – their warm-up complete, Quins head to the dressing room for some final words from their coach.

Skipper Mark McLinden looks for a gap in the Wigan defence.
(All photos: Peter Lush)

Solomon Haumono scores the second of his two tries in a dazzling display.

Luke Dorn is firmly shackled by the Wigan defence.
(Photos: Peter Lush)

Interviews and presentations

Quins chairman Ian Lenagan shares his thoughts with Chris Warren.

Left: David Hughes and Nic Cartwright – two men who kept the club going through hard times.

Below: Tony Rea pays tribute to the work of chief executive Nic Cartwright following his decision to leave the club at the end of the season.
(All photos: Peter Lush)

in extraordinary circumstances. Michael Dobson's kick-off rebounded off the Quins crossbar, straight into the arms of a grateful Bryan Fletcher, who crashed over. The home side overcame that temporary setback to go 20-6 up thanks to a Dorn try and a penalty from Henry Paul, who had already kicked three conversions. But Wigan again hit back against the run of play, Sean O'Loughlin going over. McLinden then ensured Quins finished the half on a high with a drop-goal just seconds before the interval. Not many people would have thought so at the time, but that kick was to prove crucial. However, McLinden might not have taken the shot at goal had he realised that the new scoreboards in both the East Stand and Lexus Stand were displaying the wrong time. There was in fact more than a minute left on the clock, not just a few seconds.

After the break, Hopkins scooted over for another try before the unstoppable Haumono, playing his best game of the season, brushed off several Wigan tackles for his second touchdown of the game to put Quins 31-12 up on 59 minutes. The match looked over as a contest, but Wigan were not about to lie down and die. Fletcher capped a great move for his second try, pouncing on a wonderfully weighted kick from Pat Richards, before completing his hat-trick after Neil Budworth had handed his former club possession with a bad knock-on in front of his own posts. When Dobson scored Wigan's fifth try with eight minutes left, Quins were just a point ahead and seemingly on the rack. Sensing the panic in his side and amongst the home fans, Brian McDermott left his position high up in the Lexus Stand to take a seat on the bench, a lot closer to the action. But he could only watch helplessly as Wigan continued to turn the screw. The pressure was also taking its toll on Dean Richards and Mark Evans. The coach and chief executive of NEC Harlequins were spotted with their heads in their hands as Quins' lead dwindled away. Wigan might have snatched victory, too, had a pass to Richards storming down the left touchline not been ruled forward. But Quins held on for a 31-30 win to ensure their fight for safety did not go down to the last game against Salford.

McDermott had the look of a relieved man when he sat down to answer questions from the media after the game. After joking that what little hair he had left had gone grey, he paid tribute to his team's resilience in the face of severe Wigan pressure. "It was probably not the smartest game we've played, but it was one of the gutsiest," he said. Haumono, whose rampaging runs had blasted holes in Wigan's defence all game, was singled out for special praise. "He was scary," said McDermott. "I thought he was massive for us."

The win ensured Harlequins RL would be in Super League in 2007, but McDermott was not about to write off the final match against Salford as a meaningless encounter. "We are going to keep a lid on the celebrations for now," he said. "We are breathing a little easier, but it's not about easing off the gas this week. We want to make sure we finish the season off with some good memories." McDermott also revealed that one or two players still had to convince him that they deserved a place in his squad for next season. The club had already announced that several players were leaving, but the future of several others remained undecided. "There is still a lot to play for when we take on Salford," said McDermott.

Danny Williams has nothing left to prove. A Grand Final winner with Melbourne Storm in 1999, he had made more than 200 appearances in the NRL before signing for the London Broncos at the end of 2004. He was also a former Australian Schoolboys international and had represented Ireland in the 2000 World Cup. But after 13 years of first-grade rugby, he had decided he would retire at the end of the 2006 season. "It was just the way the body was feeling," he said. "Mentally I could keep going, but it is taking longer for me to recover after each game. Anyway, all good things eventually have to come to an end."

A former team-mate of Tony Rea when they were both at North Sydney Bears, Williams arrived in London to mixed reviews. He was unquestionably talented, an inspirational leader with a big heart, but some wondered about his discipline. He had been handed an 18-match ban for striking Wests Tigers rival Mark O'Neill shortly before his move to England. In fact, he still had nine games of the suspension to serve when he signed for the Broncos. "A lot of people who have never met me think I am this crazy lunatic because of what happened," said Williams. "But once you get to know me, I'm a nice guy. I stick by my mates and if you become my friend then I'm your friend forever." It comes as little surprise to learn that Williams lists the fearsome Gorden Tallis, the former Australia second-rower who was a mainstay of the successful Brisbane Broncos and Queensland sides of the late 1990s and early 2000s, as one of his chief role models. Tallis, nicknamed the Raging Bull, was noted for his uncompromising approach to the game. "Gorden has always been the benchmark and it was a pleasure to come up against him," said Williams. "Well, maybe not a pleasure, but it was an honour to be on the same park. I'd like to think I'm someone who gives 100 per cent like he did, someone who guys want to play with rather than against. Off the field, I'd like to be

A thoughtful Danny Williams contemplates the end of his career. (Photo: Peter Lush)

remembered as someone who puts a smile on your face." Williams has earned a reputation as a joker. He can be serious and utterly professional one minute and almost slapstick the next. "I think I've got many personalities and any one of them can come out at any time," he said. "I'm usually the first to instigate something, but there's a time and a place for a joke. I like to think I get the timing right most of the time."

There have been many career highlights for Williams, but Melbourne's 1999 Grand Final victory is obviously the pick. In only their second season, the Storm were crowned NRL champions with a 20-18 defeat of St George-Illawarra Dragons in front of 107,558 fans at Sydney's Stadium Australia. Williams sees many similarities between Melbourne and London. Both clubs are rugby league outposts, set up to help spread the appeal of the game, and Williams is confident London can emulate Melbourne's success. "It hasn't won anything yet, but this is a club that is going places," he said. "Ian Lenagan's involvement is just what the doctor ordered while Brian McDermott definitely seems to be the right man for the job of coach. He is passionate and commands respect. He is also hard and fair, which means players know where they stand with him. That's important." Williams also thinks the capture of stand-off Scott Hill, his former team-mate at Melbourne, is a major coup, too. "I played seven years with him and he will be a good addition," said Williams. "He is a professional guy and a class player. The fans will appreciate his style of play and I know he is looking forward to coming over here. The big question is whether the other guys can adapt to Scott. He has so much skill that he sometimes expects too much of his team-mates. He does things that no one else is expecting and it may be hard for the other guys to keep up."

No doubt Williams would have liked to have featured alongside Hill for the Quins, but his focus will be on life after playing following his decision to quit. "I'm going to miss being around the other 25 guys in the team," said Williams. "It's going to be hard to accept that I'm never going to do that again. But I'll have a crack and a good life." Would he be emotional when the final hooter sounded against Salford? "Like a lot of guys I know, I tend to keep my emotions inside me," he said. "There may be a tear in the eye after the game, but I think it will only really hit me that I've retired a couple of weeks later."

Williams has made a big impact in his two years in the capital. Uncompromising and committed on the field, he reveals that wounds to his nose, ears, chin, mouth and scalp have accounted for more than 100 stitches since he came over here. He has also suffered several concussions, although few compare with the one he suffered earlier in his career back in Australia. "There have been many occasions when I've been dazed and not realised where I was," he said. "I remember being knocked out in one game, getting to my feet and then start playing for the opposition. I was running alongside them waiting for the ball to be passed to me. I eventually came to my senses and got on the right team again." Quins will miss Williams, and he will miss them. But he is not about to get sentimental. "People come and go, but the team will get on with the job when I'm gone," he said. "Life is all about memories and journeys, and I've got plenty of good memories."

Dorn and Williams were not the only impending departures from Harlequins RL as the 2006 season began to wind down. Scrum-half Leuluai had turned down the offer of a new contract and was on his way to Wigan while Tookey had decided to return to Australia. As for Nick Bradley-Qalilawa, Neil Budworth, Rikki Sheriffe, Paul Noone and Filimone Lolohea, they had all been told they were being released. There were some changes behind the scenes, too. Chief executive Nic Cartwright had decided the time was right to move on after eight years of service. "I feel in many ways my job is done and that it's time for a new challenge," he said. Cartwright might not always have been flavour of the month with the fans, but his loyalty to the club cannot be questioned, a fact recognised by chairman Ian Lenagan. "Communication was not Nic's greatest strength," he said. "His greatest strengths were his work-rate, his loyalty and his breadth of knowledge. He has chosen to leave because he wants a change in his work-life balance and can see there is radical change occurring to protect something he has loved for a long time – the London club." Former chairman David Hughes paid tribute to Cartwright's graft, too, adding that he had played an instrumental role "in nailing the Harlequins deal which took three years of hard graft to bring to fruition". The supporters, even those who sometimes criticised him for not listening, were quick to add their thanks, too. One wrote that Cartwright had "nothing but the best interests at heart at all times" while another added that "his heart was in the job 100 per cent and I don't think we'd be here today if it weren't for him".

The fans had a chance to say farewell in person to Cartwright, Dorn, Williams et al when Harlequins RL rounded off their season with a home game against Salford on Saturday, 16 September. It proved to be a fitting finale with a definite end-of-term feel about it. Dorn showed just what Quins would be missing by scoring a hat-trick of tries against his future employers as the home side ran out convincing 40-18 winners. There were also tries for Rob Purdham making his 100th appearance for the club, Jon Wells, Matt Gafa and Zebastian Luisi. Noone, who had been signed from Warrington on a short-term deal until the end of the season, marked his last appearance for Quins by earning a spell in the sin-bin, although he looked to be more victim than perpetrator. Salford rival Andrew Brocklehurst threw the first punch, but referee Phil Bentham only saw Noone's retaliation. The indiscretion failed to take the shine off a glittering Quins performance, which had McDermott purring with delight. "It was a very good way to end the season," he said. "I was thinking midweek that it is a long few months if you lose the last game. Now there will be some happy memories to take into the cold, dark months of pre-season."

McDermott also had a word for the players who were leaving. "I wanted to give them a good send-off," he said. "I'm sure all the boys will sit down over the next couple of days and tell each other they love each other, but at the moment they are all dancing in the dressing room. Danny Williams is even doing some air guitar. If I had been the one retiring, I would have probably smashed the dressing room up or had a fight with someone." As for those players who would be at the club next season, McDermott wasted little time reminding them of what was to come. "Part of my remit is to create a no-nonsense culture, a 'that won't do' culture," he said. "So come day one of pre-season, the slate is wiped clean and I'm Mr Nasty."

Salford vanquished - the end of the season

Jon Wells ended an injury-hit season with a try.

In his final game for Quins, Luke Dorn scored a hat-trick of tries against his future employers.

Matt Gafa goes on the attack as Quins finish the season with a 40-18 win.
(All photos: Peter Lush)

13. Dreaming of a bright future

"I have had a good relationship with the fans. I definitely have the sense that they appreciate what I have done."
David Hughes, Harlequins RL director and joint owner

David Hughes has a motto that he puts great stock in: 'Don't look back'. Had the former London Broncos chairman not heeded his own advice, he admits there is every chance he would have been carted off to the local loony bin. Hughes has poured his heart, soul and hard-earned cash into the club since taking it over in 2001. Were it not for his investment, there is little doubt it would have sunk without a trace. Just exactly how much Hughes has put in to keep the club afloat remains a mystery, but he gives three examples that highlight the magnitude of his contributions. Firstly, he says his children have expressed concern that their father is frittering away their inheritance. Secondly, he says the judge who presided over his divorce proceedings needed a lot of convincing before accepting just how much he had ploughed in. Finally, he says he will have to delay his retirement by five or six years to give him time to earn back the money he has put into the club. "Rugby league is my life, so my heart does rule my head – and my wallet," he says. "People have told me I'm mad when they find out how much I have spent on the club. But I enjoy working, so it is not such a bad thing if I don't retire when I had planned to."

Tall, with short greying hair, the affable Hughes is extremely passionate about rugby league. But his love of the Broncos, and now Harlequins RL, seems to know no bounds. Even the ring tone on his mobile telephone is 'Mighty Quinn', the theme tune of NEC Harlequins that has been successfully adopted by the rugby league club. The song is apt for Hughes in more ways than one. Not only does it signify his continuing loyalty to the club and his affection for its new identity, but also its lyrics somewhat define his own life. One of the verses eulogises that 'everybody's building ships and boats, some are building monuments, others jotting down notes'. Firstly, Hughes has plenty to do with ships and boats through his work in the oil trade. In fact, his company has just taken possession of a tanker that he has named 'Harlequin'. He has even arranged for some club tracksuits to be flown out to the ship for the crew to wear. Secondly, in Harlequins RL he is attempting to build a monument, something that will stand the test of time.

In many ways, Hughes wants Quins to replicate the success of Charlton, the top-flight football club that he is also a director of. The Addicks were once homeless and lacking direction, too. Now they are one of the game's success stories, boasting a strong community presence and mixing with the likes of Chelsea, Manchester United and Arsenal in the Premiership. "I joined the board at Charlton in 1996 when they moved back to the Valley," says Hughes. "I have had a great time there and the club is a really good example of a community club that is successful and well thought of." If Hughes had had his way, Quins would have still been playing at the Valley now. Instead, after two spells in south east London, they moved to Griffin Park in Brentford before their latest switch to the Stoop. "I was a bit frustrated we couldn't make a go of it at Charlton," says Hughes. "The problem was that, back then, Charlton were a club on the periphery of the Premiership. They went up, they came down. Some guys, including myself, wanted to turn Charlton into a sporting entity, playing rugby and football all year round. But most of the guys on the board felt it was too much of a burden. They could see the potential but argued that if Charlton got relegated the crowd might turn on them and accuse them of focusing more on the rugby than the soccer. We came to a democratic decision not to do it, but I still think we could have done a good job. It would have meant calling the rugby league club Charlton as well, but we would have had the soccer club behind us. There would have been the drive there."

Despite the hard times experienced as the Broncos, not to mention the many moves across the capital, Hughes always backed the club to the hilt. Both the Brisbane Broncos and Virgin thought they could do something with it, turn it into a viable proposition, but they failed. Yet Hughes felt there was something worth fighting for. There were times when his loyalty was pushed to the absolute limit, when he felt he was banging his head against a brick wall, but he never pulled the plug. Even if Ian Lenagan had not come along and invested both his time and money, Hughes would have carried on propping up the club, ever hopeful that the fans would suddenly start flocking to support it and thus justify his decision to keep it alive. "When Virgin pulled out, it was touch and go whether I did it on my own," said Hughes. "A lot of people said it would be tough, but the club would have folded had I not put my money in and I did not want that to happen. I kept it going. Then when the Broncos went into liquidation, I wiped off a phenomenal amount of money to make sure the club could return as the Quins."

Given that Hughes originally hails from Swinton on the outskirts of Manchester, around 200 miles from London, his love of the Quins is all the more remarkable and, some would say, harder to comprehend. Had the club always been a big part of his life, evoking happy memories of his childhood, his willingness to come to its rescue time and time again would have been all the more understandable. But it wasn't. It has only existed from 1980, when short trousers and gobstoppers were but a distant memory for Hughes. He was at that first game at Fulham in September 1980, though. Perhaps being present at the birth of a club is a far more powerful magnet, like being present at the birth of a son or daughter. You want nothing but the best for that child and take delight in watching it grow and mature. There will be times when it stumbles, but then life is not always a smooth road. In the case of Quins it has been anything but. Nevertheless, it has given Hughes memories he will cherish forever, like leading the team out for the Challenge Cup final against Leeds Rhinos in 1999. "Walking out at Wembley with Richard Branson – you never forget things like that," says Hughes. "Going to Australia for the World Club Championship was great, too. We have had some great times as well as some lows." Now, though, following the link-up with NEC Harlequins and the arrival of Ian Lenagan as chairman and joint owner, Hughes looks like he may get the rich rewards his money and loyalty deserve. The fans would certainly not begrudge him his moment in the sun. "I have enjoyed a good relationship with the supporters over the years," he says. "I definitely have the sense they appreciate what I have done. I just hope the club can become viable and successful. That is one of my big ambitions."

The move to the Twickenham Stoop and the partnership with NEC Harlequins was going to happen whether Lenagan invested in the club or not. But his arrival has certainly taken a lot of the pressure off Hughes and given the club fresh impetus. "I owned the club for several years on my own and it was too big a burden for one bloke," says Hughes, who now holds a 35 per cent stake in the club compared to Lenagan's 65 per cent slice. "Ian has made a big difference. He is helping share that burden." Hughes acknowledges that Lenagan is more than just a cash cow, though. "He wants success on the pitch and is also determined the club becomes self-sufficient," say Hughes. "Ian's big drive is to break even and then make a profit. He is certainly taking the bull by the horns."

If 2006 was an important year for Harlequins RL, then 2007 is just as crucial. Perhaps more so. With Super League moving to a franchise system in 2009, which means relegation and promotion will cease to exist in its current form, competition in the top flight is more intense than ever. "I don't think we were ever seriously threatened, but I never ever want to be in the embarrassing position of being faced by relegation again," says Lenagan. "Having the sword of Damocles hanging over your head was an awful experience." Which is why he and Hughes have approved a bigger budget for 2007.

All smiles at the end

Sylvia Waite presents Mark McLinden with the Supporters' Player of the Year trophy.

David Hughes presents Rob Purdham with a plaque to mark his 100th game for the club, which came against Salford. (Photos: Peter Lush)

Quins chairman Ian Lenagan thanks Danny Williams for two years of loyal service.

Moving on: Luke Dorn, Neil Budworth, Nick Bradley-Qalilawa, Danny Williams, Tommy Leuluai and Paul Noone.
(Photos: Peter Lush)

Mark McLinden thanks the fans for their support
at the end of a long, tough season.

Mark Tookey applauds the supporters after
his final game for the club.
(Photos: Peter Lush)

Solomon Haumono looks after his children, while
Joe Mbu reflects on the end of the season.

Head coach Brian McDermott had already started making his plans for
2007 when the 2006 season ended with the victory over Salford
(Photos: Peter Lush)

They had originally planned to spend £1.35 million but decided to increase this by a further £250,000. "We think it is a good business decision," says Lenagan. "Even if you finish bottom in 2008, you are likely to be voted back in if you have facilities like ours, so we have to make sure we are still in Super League after 2007. Quite a number of clubs have recognised that and are buying more expensive players. We have to respond accordingly."

Quins have made significant investments in their playing squad for next year. At the time this book went to press, they had signed Scott Hill, Julien Rinaldi, Sione Faumuina, Jon Grayshon, Chris Melling and David Tootill. Stand-off Hill was one of the stand-out performers in the NRL in 2006, helping Melbourne Storm reach the Grand Final. Rinaldi and Faumuina are considered exciting talents, too, while Melling, Grayshon and Tootill will all improve competition for places. "Brian has the final say but Tony, David and myself all help plan the squad," says Lenagan. "We are actually planning for 2008 and 2009, not just next season." The club is also continuing to invest heavily in its youth programme as well as sign players they think will have an immediate impact on the first team. "That is critical," says Lenagan. "I was very lucky. The first decision I ever made as chairman was to re-establish the Senior Academy. My gut instinct told me to do it. Now we have Michael Worrincy, Tony Clubb and Louie McCarthy-Scarsbrook coming through and going well." The aim of the club is to establish a "pipeline of southerners", but they recognise that such a feat is going to take five years to pull off. "In the meantime our strategy is to recruit players from the north aged 18, 19 and 20 and artificially graft them into our Academy," says Lenagan.

Other changes have been made for 2007, too, like Bill Peden's recruitment as fitness coach and conditioner. The Australian, who had one year as a player with the London Broncos in 2003, is relishing the chance to make his mark in the capital. "I'm pretty honoured to have been asked to come over," says Peden, who has spent the past three years with NRL side Newcastle Knights. "The club's vision has impressed me and I can see it going from strength to strength. It has risen out of the flames again and it's an exciting time to be involved." But perhaps the biggest change concerns Lenagan himself. When chief executive Nic Cartwright announced he would be leaving the club at the end of the 2006 season, it gave Lenagan the opportunity to be more radical in his plans for the club. For example, instead of appointing someone immediately to replace Cartwright, he opted to do the job himself. "I'm completing the restructuring and internal reorganisation of the management within the club including the appointment of finance director, business development manager and administration manager, to ensure the club's direction and momentum under the new management team are correct. A new CEO will be appointed when these have been well established in order then to kick on to the next level. It quickly became apparent when I came on board that the financial management was weak. Chris Warren and myself addressed the issue of marketing, showing we could set a high standard, but it was clear that some of the internal systems, some of the communication and some of the management was not what it should be. My job is to put the right structure in place for the future."

Few would doubt Lenagan's ability to back up his words with actions. His record in business speaks for itself. But he has already won plenty of admirers for the work he has done with Harlequins RL, among them Richard Lewis, the executive chairman of the Rugby Football League. "I have a lot of respect for Ian and what he is trying to do," says Lewis. "He is the right person to lead the club forward and everything I have heard and seen suggests this first year for the club has been a definite success." Lewis, who attended Harlequins RL's opening game against St Helens, has been a big supporter of rugby league in London. He argues that a strong presence in the capital is good for the game. But he is not the only person to highlight the fact that a lot of scepticism existed when the Quins venture was first mooted. "People were worried that the club was jumping out of the frying pan and into the fire," he says. "But once it became clear that this was going to be a partnership, the fears subsided. The word 'potential' has been used about London for a long time, but it was clear from my first meeting with people at the club that it was a great opportunity."

Lewis has first-hand knowledge of Lenagan's drive and dynamism. The Quins chairman was one of the movers and shakers behind the acceptance by the clubs of the revamping of the Super League (Europe) Ltd corporate governance structure midway through 2006. No doubt influenced by the recounted past experiences of the London Broncos, who had almost been booted out of Super League at that infamous March 2005 meeting in Huddersfield, Lenagan wanted a fairer and more objective system in place, not one that could be open to 'conflict of interest' manipulation by the clubs themselves. He backed RFL moves that would mean a 75 per cent figure could decide votes. Once the change was implemented, it was put to the test almost immediately when the 12 Super League clubs voted on the proposal to hold a complete round of games at Cardiff's Millennium Stadium in 2007. The RFL felt it would be a fantastic advertisement for the game but faced opposition from the bigger clubs, who would potentially lose money if the plan went ahead. In the end, nine clubs voted in favour of the proposal – the necessary 75 per cent figure - and a complete round of six games will indeed be staged in the Welsh capital on 5 and 6 May 2007.

It is fair to say that not many Harlequins RL fans knew who Lenagan was when he took over, let alone what his hopes and aspirations were for the club. They know a lot more now. They seem to like and respect him, too. They believe he has the club's best interests at heart and see sense in most of the decisions he has taken. "He is a breath of fresh air at boardroom level," says Quins fan Ron Knox. "He is very assertive, very decisive and knows how to make things happen. He is a dominant figure who leads from the front and is exactly what this organisation has been looking for." Knox applauds the changes Lenagan has already implemented as well as his plans to further improve management and administration at the club. But perhaps what most impresses Knox – and no doubt fans in general - is Lenagan's desire to get to know the supporters better. "Supporters don't expect to be told confidential information, but they do want to know what the club's aims and ambitions are," says Knox. "Ian is trying to bridge the gap that exists between the club and its fans. He talks to them and reads what they have to say on the internet messageboards, so he knows what they are thinking. If there is a concerted view, then he will act on it."

A committed league fan, Knox has bought into the whole Harlequins ethos, buying an NEC Harlequins season ticket and going a long way to embracing the union game. While that may be a step too far for a lot of ex-London Broncos supporters, it is fair to say that most of them have warmed to the idea that their team is now called Harlequins and wears the pastel colours made famous by the rival code. Some diehard Broncos fans have even bought a Harlequins RL shirt, though in quite a few instances they have opted for the away top rather than the home one. The affinity with the Quins brand will only increase, too. The supporters seem happy shouting 'Har-lee-quins' or 'We're Quins RL', while the atmosphere at the Stoop noticeably improved as the season wore on. "It took a while for fans to adapt, but then it was always going to," says Knox. "You can't expect them to suddenly start chanting another name. Fans are more tribal than that." But the signs are good.

Ultimately, success on the pitch is what counts and is what will convince most former Broncos fans that the link-up with NEC Harlequins was the right one. Lenagan knows that, too. "We want to win something quickly, in the next couple of years, and we want to be pulling in 10,000 spectators," he says. It is a bold statement, but then we have come to expect nothing less. The man charged with bringing a trophy or two to the club is head coach Brian

McDermott. It was a calculated risk appointing him with just eight matches remaining and relegation still a big concern. But the former Royal Marine threw himself into the job with typical gusto. It may be too early to judge whether he is as good as everyone says and expects him to be, but he has made a positive start. In one aspect bringing him in towards the tail end of the season was a good move. It allowed him to assess the squad and make changes before the off-season, when it would have been harder to make a judgment call on a player and identify areas of weakness. "In many ways it was scary to come in with a possible relegation looming," he admits. "I would have been the one to get the blame if we had gone down. But coming in at the coalface, I found out what people are like and I found out a bit about myself as well."

Harlequins RL ended up avoiding relegation by beating Wigan in their penultimate game of the season. It was another typical roller-coaster year for the London club, punctuated by a few highs, like the draw at Odsal and the wins at Hull, Wigan and Salford, but many more lows, notably the defeats at Castleford and Catalans Dragons in the second half of the season. One minute the play-offs looked within reach. The next Quins looked down and out, needing other clubs to slip up if they were to avoid the dreaded drop into the National League. The implications for the club had it been relegated do not bear thinking about. Ironically, after their disastrous start at home – they lost their first four games - Quins won 10 of their last 12 matches at the Twickenham Stoop, chalking up victories over Bradford, Warrington, Salford and Hull, who all made the play-offs. Had they started as well as they finished, Quins might have made the top six themselves instead of finishing seventh. Attendances at the Stoop would probably have been so much better, too. But, as Hughes says, it is pointless to look back and wonder what might have been. Interestingly, RFL chief Lewis believes the club may have been better served by not getting off to a flying start at home. He argues that the club needs to focus on "sustainable" growth, adding that a "slow burn" is better than a "boom-then-bust" scenario. He may be right, but they can ill afford another poor start in 2007.

It is hard to judge whether 2006 was a success or not for Harlequins RL. It was a landmark year, but is only the start of what will hopefully be a bright and trophy-laden future at the Stoop. The partnership with NEC Harlequins is initially due to run for three years, although the option for a further two is almost certain to be taken. That gives the club time to establish itself in a part of London where it feels at home. The fans hope this is the last move. Tired, jaded and a little cynical from travelling around the capital, they want to make TW2 7SX their permanent residence.

Appendix: Statistics and records

The 2006 season: Match by match record

11 February: Harlequins RL 16 St Helens 40
Quins: Gafa, Sheriffe, Luisi, Smith, Bradley-Qalilawa, Dorn, Leuluai, Temata, Weisner, Heckenberg, Purdham, Hopkins, Williams. *Subs:* Haumono, Mills, Sykes, Tookey.
Tries: Smith, Sheriffe, Sykes. *Goals:* Gafa, Sykes.
Saints: Wellens, Gardner, Lyon, Talau, Meli, Pryce, Long, Fozzard, Cunningham, Cayless, Gilmour, Wilkin, Hooper. *Subs*: Roby, Graham, P. Anderson, Fa'asavalu.
Tries: Wellens 3, Cayless, Gardner, Hooper, Lyon. *Goals:* Lyon 6.
Attendance: 8,213

18 February: Bradford Bulls 18 Harlequins RL 18
Bulls: Withers, Bai, B. Harris, Hape, Price, I. Harris, Deacon, Fielden, Henderson, Lynch, Meyers, Johnson, Langley. *Subs:* Vagana, McKenna, Gene, Cook.
Tries: Henderson, Hape, B. Harris; *Goals:* Deacon 3.
Quins: Luisi, Sheriffe, Purdham, Sykes, Bradley-Qalilawa, Gafa, Leuluai, Temata, Weisner, Heckenberg, Haumono, Hopkins, Mbu. *Subs:* Williams, Mills, Tookey, Clubb.
Tries: Leuluai, Williams, Hopkins; *Goals:* Sykes 3.
Attendance: 11,097.

25 February: Harlequins RL 6 Wakefield Trinity Wildcats 26
Quins: Luisi, Bradley-Qalilawa, Sykes, Purdham, Clubb, Gafa, Leuluai, Temata, Weisner, Heckenberg, Haumono, Hopkins, Mbu. *Subs:* Williams, Smith, Tookey, Mills.
Try: Tookey; *Goal:* Sykes.
Wildcats: Halpenny, White, Demetriou, Whittle, Tadulala, Obst, Jeffries, Catic, March, MacGillivray, Solomona, Elima, Betham. *Subs:* Griffin, Applegarth, Korkidas, Saxton.
Tries: Tadulala 3, Obst, Halpenny; *Goals:* Jeffries 2, March.
Attendance: 3,554

3 March: Hull 6 Harlequins RL 10
Hull: Briscoe, Tony, Domic, Yeaman, Raynor, Horne, Brough, Dowes, Swain, King, Radford, McMenemy, Cooke. *Subs:* Thackray, Carvell, Chester, Whiting.
Try: Briscoe; Goal*:* Brough.
Quins: Luisi, Gafa, Sykes, Smith, Bradley-Qalilawa, Dorn, Leuluai, Mills, Weisner, Tookey, Purdham, Hopkins, Temata. *Subs:* Williams, Haumono, Heckenberg, Lolohea.
Tries: Leuluai, Smith; *Goal:* Sykes.
Attendance: 8,250

12 March: Harlequins RL 20 Castleford Tigers 34
Quins: Luisi, Bradley-Qalilawa, Clubb, Smith, Gafa, Dorn, Leuluai, Tookey, Weisner, Heckenberg, Purdham, Hopkins, Temata. *Subs:* Williams, Haumono, Mills, Lolohea.
Tries: Hopkins 2, Clubb, Leuluai; *Goals:* Gafa 2.
Tigers: Platt, Pryce, Shenton, Bird, Viane, McGoldrick, Kain, Sculthorpe, Henderson, Nutley, Fletcher, Whittaker, Fa'aoso. *Subs:* Handforth, Huby, Ward, Dyer.
Tries: Pryce, Shenton, McGoldrick, Sculthorpe, Fletcher, Handforth; *Goals:* Huby 5.
Attendance: 3,535.

19 March: Huddersfield Giants 64 Harlequins RL 14
Giants: Reilly, Donlan, Evans, Torrens, Gardner, Thorman, Paul, Crabtree, Drew, Jackson, Nero, Jones, Wild. *Subs:* Snitch, March, McDonald, Raleigh.
Tries: Evans 2, Thorman 2, Gardner 2, Donlan, Wild, Paul, Crabtree, Torrens; *Goals:* Thorman 10.
Quins: Luisi, Gafa, Hartley, Smith, Bradley-Qalilawa, Dorn, Leuluai, Tookey, Randall, Lolohea, Temata, Hopkins, Williams. *Subs:* Budworth, Mills, Heckenberg, Clubb.
Tries: Hartley, Luisi. *Goals:* Gafa 3.
Attendance: 4,173.

25 March: Harlequins RL 0 Leeds 60
Quins: Dorn, Bradley-Qalilawa, Hartley, Smith, Gafa, Weisner, Leuluai, Tookey, Randall, Lolohea, Mbu, Hopkins, Williams. *Subs:* Budworth, Heckenberg, Mills, McCarthy-Scarsbrook.
Leeds: Mathers, Donald, Ellis, Senior, Smith, McGuire, Burrow, Peacock, Diskin, Feather, Poching, Kirke, Sinfield, *Subs*: Millard, Lauitiiti, Bailey, Scruton.
Tries: McGuire 4, Burrow, Poching, Smith, Lauitiiti, Feather, Senior. *Goals:* Sinfield 9, Burrow.
Attendance: 5,208

2 April: Harlequins RL 48 Toulouse 6 (Challenge Cup 4)
Quins: McLinden, Clubb, Gafa, Smith, Bradley-Qalilawa, Dorn, Leuluai, Tookey, Randall, Heckenberg, Haumono, Hopkins, Williams. *Subs:* Mills, McCarthy-Scarsbrook, Budworth, Weisner.
Tries: Clubb 3, Dorn 2, Smith, Gafa, Leuluai, Bradley-Qalilawa; *Goals:* Gafa 6.
Toulouse: Clayton, Olieu, Houles, Viala, Lima, Myles, Wynne, Prizzon, Gay, McDonald, Vincent, Raguin, Delpoux. *Subs:* Arcas, Frayssinet, Howell, Amigasa.
Try: Myles; *Goal:* Wynne
Attendance: 1,245.

7 April: St Helens 16 Harlequins RL 6
St Helens: Wellens, Gardner, Lyon, Talau, Meli, Pryce, Long, Anderson, Cunningham, Fozzard, Gilmour, Sculthorpe, Hooper. *Subs:* Roby, Wilkin, Graham, Fa'asavki.
Tries: Wellens, Gardner, Graham. *Goals:* Lyon 2.
Quins: McLinden, Clubb, Gafa, Smith, Bradley-Qalilawa, Dorn, Leuluai, Tookey, Weisner, Heckenberg, Williams, Hopkins, Mbu. *Subs:* Budworth, Mills, Sheriffe, McCarthy-Scarsbrook.
Try: McLinden; *Goal:* Gafa.
Attendance: 9,520

14 April: Harlequins RL 36 Catalans Dragons 14
Quins: McLinden, Gafa, Luisi, Smith, Bradley-Qalilawa, Dorn, Leuluai, Heckenberg, Randall, Tookey, Purdham, Hopkins, Williams. *Subs:* Mills, Budworth, Weisner, McCarthy-Scarsbrook.
Tries: Dorn 2, Luisi, Purdham, Leuluai, Williams, McCarthy-Scarsbrook.
Goals: Gafa 4.
Catalans Dragons: Guigue, Murphy, Touxagas, Hughes, Verges, Rudder, Dobson, Beattie, Rinaldi, Guisset, Fakir, Mounis, Wilson. *Subs:* Jampy, Berthezene, Fellous, Casty.
Tries: Rudder, Hughes, Wilson. Goal*:* Rinaldi
Attendance: 3,472.

17 April: Wigan Warriors 18 Harlequins RL 30
Warriors: Moran, Ashton, Gleeson, Richards, Dallas, Brown, Orr, Higham, Hargreaves, Wilkes, Tickle, Jonkers, O'Loughlin. *Subs:* Godwin, James, Palea'aesina, O'Carroll.
Tries: Moran, Brown, O'Loughlin, James; Goal*:* Tickle.
Quins: McLinden, Sheriffe, Smith, Gafa, Bradley-Qalilawa, Dorn, Leuluai, Mills, Randall, Heckenberg, Purdham, Hopkins, Mbu. *Subs:* Williams, Luisi, Tookey, Budworth.
Tries: Dorn 2, Sheriffe, Smith Gafa, Mills; *Goals:* Purdham 2, Gafa.
Attendance: 12,329.

23 April: Wakefield Trinity Wildcats 42 Harlequins RL 22
Wildcats: Saxton, Halpenny, Atkins, Demetriou, Tadulala, Rooney, Jeffries, MacGillivray, Obst, Korkidas, Solomona, Field, Betham. *Subs:* White, Griffin, White, Catic.
Tries: Rooney 2, Halpenny, Atkins, Demetriou, Tadulala, White; *Goals:* Rooney 7.
Quins: McLinden, Clubb, Luisi, Smith, Bradley-Qalilawa, Dorn, Leuluai, Mills, Randall, Heckenberg, Purdham, Hopkins, Mbu. *Subs:* Tookey, Haumono, Budworth, Temata.
Tries: Leuluai 2, Dorn, McLinden; *Goals;* Purdham 3.
Attendance: 3,527.

29 April: Harlequins RL 22 Huddersfield Giants 16
Quins: McLinden, Lucky Luisi, Smith, Purdham, Bradley-Qalilawa, Dorn, Leuluai, Temata, Randall, Tookey, Haumono, Hopkins, Williams. *Subs:* Mbu, Budworth, Mills, H. Paul.
Tries: Tries*:* Bradley-Qalilawa 2, McLinden, Mills; *Goals:* Purdham 2, Paul.
Giants: Reilly, Aspinwall, Evans, De Vere, Donlan, March, R. Paul, Jackson, Drew, Gannon, Nero, Jones, Wild. *Subs:* Crabtree, Smith, Raleigh, Hemingway.
Tries: Tries*:* Jones, Evans, Donlan; *Goals:* De Vere 2.
Attendance: 12,000 (This was the attendance for both the rugby union and rugby league matches. The attendance for the rugby league match was around 7,000).

5 May: Leeds Rhinos 36 Harlequins RL 24
Rhinos: Mathers, Donald, Gibson, Senior, Smith, McGuire, Burrow, Peacock, Diskin, Feather, Walker, Jones-Buchanan, Ellis. *Subs:* Millard, O'Neill, Scruton, Poching.
Tries: Diskin 2, McGuire, Poching, Donald, Peacock; *Goals:* Burrow 6.
Quins: McLinden, Gafa, Luisi, Smith, Bradley-Qalilawa, Paul, Dorn, Tookey, Randall, Mills, Hopkins, Purdham, Haumono. *Subs:* Williams, Lolohea, Weisner, Budworth.
Tries: McLinden 2, Smith, Dorn; *Goals:* Paul 4.
Attendance: 12,301

13 May: Harlequins RL 16 Bradford Bulls 58
Quins: McLinden, Luisi, Gafa, Smith, Bradley-Qalilawa, Paul, Dorn, Lolohea, Budworth, Mills, Hopkins, Purdham, Mbu. *Subs:* Williams, Worrincy, Tookey, Randall.
Tries: McLinden, Hopkins, Luisi. *Goals:* Paul 2.
Bulls: St Hilaire, Bai, B. Harris, Hape, Vainikolo, I. Harris, Deacon, Fielden, Newton, Lynch, Ferres, Johnson, Langley. *Subs:* Pryce, Gene, Henderson, Vagana.
Tries: Vainikolo 2, Lynch 2, Hape 2, St Hilaire, Bai, Fielden, Pryce. *Goals:* Deacon 9.
Attendance: 4,491

20 May: Harlequins RL 82 Barrow Raiders 8 (Challenge Cup 5)
Quins: Luisi, Smith, Gafa, Purdham, Bradley-Qalilawa, Weisner, Dorn, Tookey, Randall, Mills, Hopkins, Worrincy, Mbu. *Subs:* Lolohea, Budworth, Hartley, Williams (did not play).
Tries: Dorn 2, Worrincy 2, Weisner 2, Purdham 2, Mbu, Randall, Hopkins, Gafa, Bradley-Qalilawa, Hartley; *Goals:* Purdham 13.
Raiders: Jones, Finch, Atkinson, Harris, Nixon, Kaighan, Holt, Raftery, Archer, Blake, McDermott, Wilcock, Whitehead. *Subs:* Marshall, Luxon, Butler, Wood.
Tries: Finch, Nixon.
Attendance: 1,512

29 May: Salford City Reds 28 Harlequins RL 29
City Reds: Myler, Hodgson, Littler, Moule, Stewart, Dunemann, Robinson, Rutgerson, Alker, Highton, Coley, Sibbit, Finnigan; *Subs:* Langi, Charles, Clayton, Haggerty.
Tries: Littler 3, Sibbit, Haggerty; *Goals:* Myler 4.
Quins: McLinden, Smith, Luisi, Gafa, Bradley-Qalilawa, Paul, Dorn, Tookey, Randall, Williams, Hopkins, Purdham, Mbu. *Subs:* Haumono, Mills, Weisner, Worrincy.
Tries: Williams, Hopkins, McLinden, Weisner, Haumono; *Goals:* Purdham 4; *Drop-goal:* Paul.
Attendance: 3,295

4 June: Leeds Rhinos 36 Harlequins RL 18 (Challenge Cup 6)
Rhinos: Smith, Donald, Walker, Senior, Williams, McGuire, Burrow, Jones-Buchanan, Diskin, Scruton, Peacock, Ellis, Sinfield. *Subs:* O'Neill, Millard, Lauitiiti, Poching.
Tries: Poching, Williams 3, Donald 2, McGuire. *Goals:* Sinfield 4.
Quins: McLinden, Smith, Luisi, Purdham, Bradley-Qalilawa, Paul, Dorn, Tookey, Randall, Lolohea, Haumono, Hopkins, Mbu. *Subs:* Williams, Mills, Weisner, Worrincy.
Tries: Dorn, Worrincy, Weisner, Smith. *Goal:* Purdham.
Attendance: 5,332

10 June: Harlequins RL 30 Warrington Wolves 28
Quins: Paul, Smith, Luisi, Purdham, Bradley-Qalilawa, Weisner, Dorn, Temata, Randall, Mills, Worrincy, Haumono, Mbu. *Subs:* Tookey, Heckenberg, Lolohea, Budworth.
Tries: Worrincy, Purdham, Weisner, Paul, Haumono. *Goals:* Paul 5.
Wolves: Grose, Fa'afili, Martin Gleeson, Kohe-Love, Barnett, Briers, Bridge, Leikvoll, Clarke, Wood, Wainwright, Swann, Westwood. *Subs:* Mark Gleeson, Lima, Hilton, Grix.
Tries: Briers, Swann, Barnett, Grix 2. *Goals:* Briers 4.
Attendance: 3,691

16 June: Hull 30 Harlequins RL 16
Hull: Tony, Blacklock, Domic, Whiting, Dixon, Cooke, R. Horne, Dowes, Swain, Carvell, Radford, McMenemy, Washbrook. *Subs:* G. Horne, King, Lee, Wheeldon.
Tries: R. Horne 2, Tony, Whiting, G. Horne. *Goals:* Cooke 5.
Quins: Paul, Wells, Luisi, Smith, Bradley-Qalilawa, Weisner, Dorn, Temata, Randall, Mills, Purdham, Haumono, Mbu. *Subs:* Tookey, Heckenberg, Lolohea, Budworth.
Tries: Dorn 2, Randall. *Goals:* Paul 2.
Attendance: 9,540

24 June: Catalans Dragons 38 Harlequins RL 18
Catalans Dragons: Guigue, Murphy, Wilson, Hughes, Verges, Rudder, Jones, Beattie, Cologni, Fellous, Guisset, Fakir, Mounis. *Subs:* Berthezene, Frayssinous, Chan, Casty.
Tries: Murphy 2, Mounis, Verges, Cologni, Hughes. *Goals:* Jones 7.
Quins: McLinden, Wells, Luisi, Smith, Bradley-Qalilawa, Paul, Dorn, Tookey, Randall, Temata, Haumono, Purdham, Williams. *Subs:* Budworth, Mills, Heckenberg, Weisner.
Tries: Bradley-Qalilawa, Temata, Smith. *Goals:* Paul 3.
Attendance: 4,197

1 July: Harlequins RL 24 Wigan Warriors 26
Quins: Luisi, Wells, Gafa, Smith, Bradley-Qalilawa, Paul, McLinden, Temata, Randall, Tookey, Haumono, Purdham, Mbu. *Subs:* Weisner, Williams, Leuluai, Heckenberg.
Tries: Haumono, Weisner (penalty try), Mbu, McLinden. *Goals:* Paul 4.
Warriors: Ashton, Calderwood, Radlinski, McAvoy, Dallas, Orr, Dobson, Fielden, Higham, Paleaaesina, Hock, Fletcher, O'Loughlin. *Subs:* Logan, O'Carroll, Hansen, Tickle.
Tries: Ashton 2, Dallas, Calderwood. *Goals:* Dobson 5.
Attendance: 4,114.

8 July: Harlequins RL 24 Castleford Tigers 16
Quins: McLinden, Smith, Gafa, Luisi, Bradley-Qalilawa, Paul, Weisner, Mills, Randall, Heckenberg, Purdham, Hopkins, Mbu. *Subs:* Tookey, Budworth, Lolohea, McCarthy-Scarsbrook.
Tries: McLinden 2, Hopkins, Randall. *Goals:* Paul 4.
Tigers: Platt, Pryce, Viane, Shenton, A. Fletcher, Brough, Lupton, Sculthorpe, Henderson, Nutley, R. Fletcher, Ward, Roarty. *Subs:* Fa'aoso, Manu, Huby, Handforth.
Tries: Manu, Huby, Viane. *Goals:* Brough 2.
Attendance: 3,656

14 July: St Helens 30 Harlequins RL 24
Saints: Wellens, Gardner, Lyon, Gilmour, V. Anderson, Pryce, Smith, Cayless, Cunningham, P. Anderson, Wilkin, Graham, Hooper. *Subs:* Roby, Fozzard, Hardman, Fa'asavalu.
Tries: Smith, Cunningham, Fozzard, Graham, Gardner; *Goals:* Lyon 5.
Quins: McLinden, Smith, Gafa, Luisi, Bradley-Qalilawa, Dorn, Leuluai, Mills, Randall, Heckenberg, Purdham, Hopkins, Paul. *Subs:* Budworth, Weisner, Mbu, Tookey.
Tries: Heckenberg, Smith, Bradley-Qalilawa, McLinden; *Goals:* Paul 4.
Attendance: 7,950

22 July: Harlequins RL 18 Hull 16
Quins: McLinden, Wells, Gafa, Smith, Bradley-Qalilawa, Dorn, Leuluai, Mills, Randall, Heckenberg, Purdham, Hopkins, Paul. *Subs:* Worrincy, Budworth, Tookey, Noone.
Tries: McLinden 3; *Goals:* Purdham 2, Paul.
Hull: Briscoe, Blacklock, Tony, Domic, Dixon, R. Horne, Lee, Dowes, Swain, King, Radford, McMenemy, Washbrook. *Subs:* G. Horne, Chester, Higgins, Wheeldon.
Tries: Blacklock, Tony, Domic; *Goals:* Dixon 2.
Attendance: 4,023

4 August: Salford City Reds 34 Harlequins RL 0
City Reds: Fitzpatrick, Hodgson, McGuinness, Moule, Langi, Dunemann, Robinson, Rutgerson, Alker, Lima, Coley, Littler, Charles. *Subs:* Highton, Haggerty, Gower, Wilshere.
Tries: Rutgerson, Robinson, McGuinness, Haggerty, Coley, Moule; *Goals:* Hodgson 5.
Quins: McLinden, Wells, Gafa, Smith, Bradley-Qalilawa, Dorn, Leuluai, Mills, Randall, Heckenberg, Noone, Hopkins, Paul. *Subs:* Williams, Haumono, Budworth, Tookey.
Attendance: 3,046

12 August: Harlequins RL 28 Bradford Bulls 26
Quins: Sykes, Stewart, Gafa, Smith, Bradley-Qalilawa, Paul, Dorn, Mills, Randall, Heckenberg, Hopkins, Noone, Purdham. *Subs:* Budworth, Williams, Haumono, Tookey.
Tries: Randall 2, Dorn, Hopkins, Smith. *Goals:* Paul 4.
Bulls: St Hilaire, Vainikolo, Hape, B. Harris, Bai, I. Harris, Deacon, Vagana, Newton, Lynch, McKenna, Ferres, Langley. *Subs:* Gene, Meyers, Withers, Henderson.
Tries: Vainikolo, Bai, Hape, Deacon, Ferres. *Goals:* Deacon 3.
Attendance: 3,793

19 August: Warrington Wolves 28 Harlequins RL 22
Wolves: Reardon, Fa'afili, Martin Gleeson, Kohe-Love, Grose, Bridge, Briers, Leikvoll, Sullivan, Rauhihi, Swann, Wainwright, Westwood. *Subs:* Mark Gleeson, Barnett, Wood, Bracek.
Tries: Bridge, Fa'afili, Kohe-Love, Bracek, M. Gleeson. *Goals:* Briers 4.
Quins: Sykes, Stewart, Smith, Gafa, Bradley-Qalilawa, Paul, Dorn, Heckenberg, Randall, Mills, Hopkins, Noone, Purdham. *Subs:* Budworth, Haumono, Williams, Tookey.
Tries: Bradley-Qalilawa 2, Haumono, Randall; *Goals:* Paul 2, Sykes 1.
Attendance: 7,375

2 September: Castleford Tigers 27 Harlequins RL 12
Tigers: Platt, A. Fletcher, Shenton, McGoldrick, Dyer, Lupton, Brough, Sculthorpe, Henderson, Nutley, Manu, Ward, R. Fletcher. *Subs:* Bird, Viane, Fa'aoso, Davis.
Tries: Dyer, McGoldrick, Lupton, Manu. *Goals*: Brough 3. *Drop-goal*: Sculthorpe.
Quins: McLinden, Stewart, Luisi, Smith, Bradley-Qalilawa, Sykes, Dorn, Mills, Randall, Heckenberg, Purdham, Hopkins, Paul. *Subs:* Williams, Haumono, Noone, Budworth.
Tries: Sykes, Williams. *Goals*: Sykes 2.
Attendance: 5,531

10 September: Harlequins RL 31 Wigan Warriors 30
Quins: McLinden, Gafa, Smith, Luisi, Stewart, Paul, Dorn, Heckenberg, Randall, Haumono, Purdham, Hopkins, Noone. *Subs*: Budworth, Williams, Mills, Leuluai
Tries: Hopkins 2, Haumono 2, Dorn. *Goals*: Paul 5; Drop-goal: McLinden.
Warriors: Ashton, Calderwood, Vaealiki, McAvoy, Richards, Orr, Dobson, Fielden, Higham, Palea'aesina, Hock, Fletcher, O'Loughlin. *Subs:* Logan, Tickle, Godwin, Hansen.
Tries: Fletcher 3, O'Loughlin, Dobson. *Goals*: Dobson 5.
Attendance: 5,737

16 September: Harlequins RL 40 Salford City Reds 18
Quins: Luisi, Bradley-Qalilawa, Smith, Gafa, Wells, Dorn, McLinden, Tookey, Budworth, Haumono, Purdham, Noone, Williams. *Subs:* Heckenberg, Randall, Sykes, Mills.
Tries: Dorn 3, Purdham, Wells, Gafa, Luisi. *Goals*: Purdham 6.
City Reds: Hodgson, Wilshire, Moule, Littler, McGuinness, Dunemann, Robinson, Rutgerson, Alker, Highton, Coley, Brocklehurst, Finnigan. *Subs:* Turner, Haggerty, Charles, Adamson.
Tries: Robinson, Hodgson, Charles. *Goals*: Charles 3.
Attendance: 3,053

Player records 2006

	Super League					Challenge Cup				Overall totals				
	A	S	T	G	DG	A	S	T	G	A	S	T	G	DG
N. Bradley-Qalilawa	27	0	6	0	0	3	0	2	0	30	0	8	0	0
N. Budworth	2	19	0	0	0	0	2	0	0	2	21	0	0	0
T. Clubb	4	2	1	0	0	1	0	3	0	5	2	4	0	0
L. Dorn	24	0	13	0	0	3	0	5	0	27	0	18	0	0
M. Gafa	22	0	2	12	0	2	0	2	6	24	0	4	18	0
T. Hartley	2	0	1	0	0	0	1	1	0	2	1	2	0	0
S. Haumono	10	9	6	0	0	2	0	0	0	12	9	6	0	0
D. Heckenberg	16	8	1	0	0	1	0	0	0	17	8	1	0	0
L. Hopkins	23	0	9	0	0	3	0	1	0	26	0	10	0	0
T. Leuluai	15	2	6	0	0	1	0	1	0	16	2	7	0	0
F. Lolohea	3	6	0	0	0	1	1	0	0	4	7	0	0	0
Z. Luisi	21	1	4	0	0	2	0	0	0	23	1	4	0	0
L. McCarthy-Scarsbrook	0	4	1	0	0	0	1	0	0	0	5	1	0	0
M. McLinden	17	0	14	0	1	2	0	0	0	19	0	14	0	1
D. Mills	14	13	2	0	0	1	2	0	0	15	15	2	0	0
J. Mbu	12	2	1	0	0	2	0	1	0	14	2	2	0	0
P. Noone	5	2	0	0	0	0	0	0	0	5	2	0	0	0
H. Paul	15	1	1	41	1	1	0	0	0	16	1	1	41	1
R. Purdham	24	0	3	19	0	2	0	2	14	26	0	5	33	0
C. Randall	20	2	5	0	0	3	0	1	0	23	2	6	0	0
R. Sheriffe	3	1	2	0	0	0	0	0	0	3	1	2	0	0
T. Smith	26	1	7	0	0	3	0	2	0	29	1	9	0	0
A. Stewart	4	0	0	0	0	0	0	0	0	4	0	0	0	0
P. Sykes	6	2	2	9	0	0	0	0	0	6	2	2	9	0
K. Temata	11	1	1	0	0	0	0	0	0	11	1	1	0	0
M. Tookey	12	14	1	0	0	3	0	0	0	15	14	1	0	0
P. Weisner	10	6	3	0	0	1	2	3	0	11	8	6	0	0
J. Wells	6	0	1	0	0	0	0	0	0	6	0	1	0	0
D. Williams	9	13	4	0	0	1	1	0	0	10	14	4	0	0
M. Worrincy	1	3	1	0	0	1	1	3	0	2	4	4	0	0
Totals			98	81	2			27	20			125	101	2

Key:
A: Appearances; S: Substitute appearances where played; T: Tries;
G: Goals; DG: Drop-goals.

- 12 players made their first team debuts.
- 30 players played for Harlequins RL.
- 26 players scored tries for Harlequins RL.
- The top try scorer was Luke Dorn with 20.
- The top goal-kicker was Henry Paul with 42.
- Only two players scored drop-goals: Henry Paul and Mark McLinden.

Super League final table 2006

	P	W	D	L	F	A	Pts
St Helens	28	24	0	4	939	430	48
Hull FC	28	20	0	8	720	578	40
Leeds Rhinos	28	19	0	9	869	543	38
Bradford Bulls*	28	16	2	10	802	568	32
Salford City Reds	28	13	0	15	600	539	26
Warrington Wolves	28	13	0	15	743	721	26
Harlequins RL	28	11	1	16	556	823	23
Wigan Warriors*	28	12	0	16	644	715	22
Huddersfield Giants	28	11	0	17	609	753	22
Wakefield Trinity Wildcats	28	10	0	18	591	717	20
Castleford Tigers	28	9	1	18	575	968	19
Catalans Dragons	28	8	0	20	601	894	16

*2 points deducted for 2005 salary cap breaches

Club records

Honours:

Super League runners up 1997
Challenge Cup runners up 1999
Division Two champions 1982-83
Division Two promoted 1980-81
Divisional Premiership runners up 1993-94

Highest score:

82-0 versus Highfield 12 November 1995 (Regal Trophy)
82-8 versus Barrow Raiders 20 May 2006 (Challenge Cup)
72-8 versus Wakefield Trinity Wildcats 27 February 2005 (Super League)

Record attendance:

15,013 versus Wakefield Trinity 15 February 1981
(Challenge Cup at Craven Cottage)

Individual records:

Most tries in first team match:
5: Martin Offiah versus Whitehaven 14 March 1999 (Challenge Cup)
Greg Barwick, Karle Hammond, Rob Purdham and Luke Dorn have all scored four tries in a Super League match.

Most tries in season:
43 by Mark Johnson in 1993-94.
In Super League: 24 by Dennis Moran in 2003.

Most tries for the club:
86 by Scott Roskell 1992 to 1997.
In Super League: 74 by Dennis Moran 2001 to 2004

Most goals in first team match:
13 by Rob Purdham versus Barrow Raiders 20 May 2006
In Super League: 12 by Paul Sykes versus Wakefield Trinity 27 February 2005.

Most goals in a season:
159 by John Gallagher in 1993-94.
In Super League: 120 by Paul Sykes in 2005

Most goals for first team:
309 by Steve Diamond 1981 to 1984

Most goals in Super League matches:
229 by Paul Sykes 2001 to 2006

Most points in first team match:
34 by Rob Purdham versus Barrow Raiders 20 May 2006 (Challenge Cup)
In Super League match: 28 by Greg Barwick versus Castleford on 25 August 1996.

Most points in season:
384 by John Gallagher in 1993-94

Most points in Super League matches in a season:
290 by Paul Sykes in 2005. (His overall total for the season was 324)

Most points for first team:
691 by Steve Diamond from 1981 to 1984.

Most points in Super League matches:
573 by Paul Sykes from 2001 to 2006.

Most first team appearances:
202 by Steele Retchless from 1998 to 2004.

Other books on rugby league in London

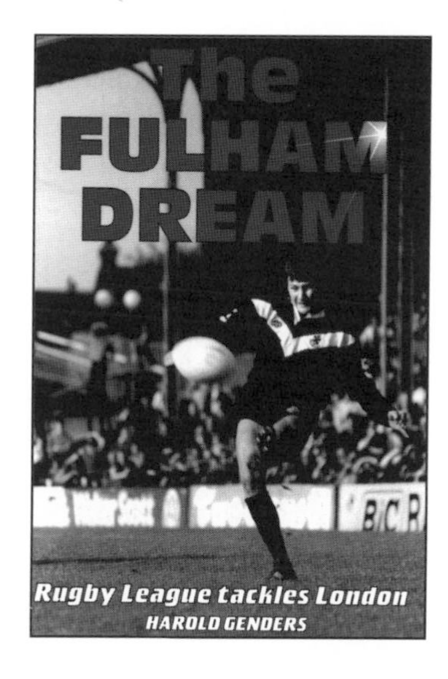

From Fulham to Wembley: Published in 2000 to mark the club's 20th anniversary. Memories from players, coaches, officials and supporters.

The Fulham Dream: Harold Genders on how he launched the club, recruited the players and the team won promotion in their first season.

I, George Nepia: New edition of autobiography of New Zealand rugby legend who played for Streatham & Mitcham in the 1930s.

£5 each or £15 for all 3. Credit card orders via www.llpshop.co.uk or by cheque to London League Publications Ltd, PO Box 10441, London E14 8WR.

More books on rugby league

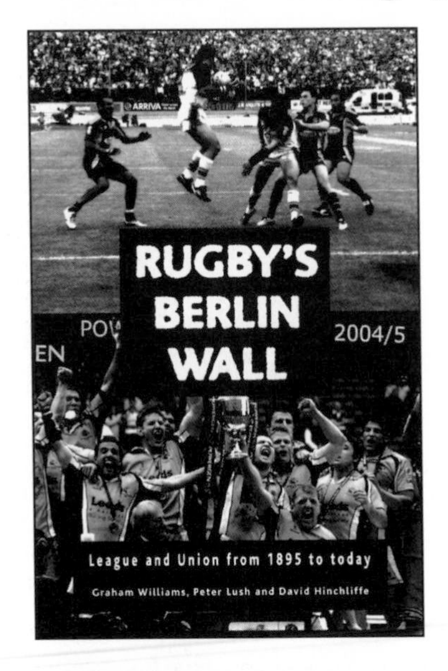

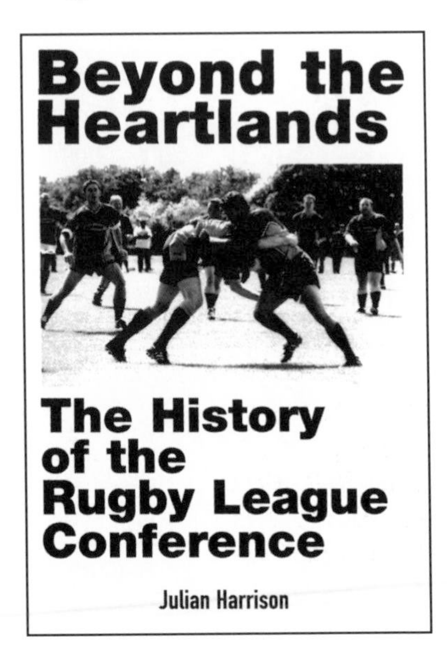

Rugby's Berlin Wall by Graham Williams, Peter Lush and David Hinchliffe looks at the relationship between League and Union from 1895 to today. £11.95

Beyond the Heartlands by Julian Harrison is the inside story of the formation and development of the Rugby League Conference. £5 special offer.

We'll Support You Evermore by David Kuzio – fans' memories of the game. £11.95.

Credit card orders via www.llpshop.co.uk or by cheque to London League Publications Ltd, PO Box 10441, London E14 8WR.